T0286362

# *the* wisdom codes
## codes

# ALSO BY GREGG BRADEN

## Books

*Human by Design/The Science of Self-Empowerment*
*Resilience from the Heart*
*The Turning Point*
*Deep Truth*
*The Divine Matrix*
*Fractal Time*
*The God Code*
*Secrets of the Lost Mode of Prayer*
*The Spontaneous Healing of Belief*
*The Isaiah Effect\**

## Audio Programs

*An Ancient Magical Prayer* (with Deepak Chopra)
*The Turning Point*
*Awakening the Power of a Modern God*
*Deep Truth*
*The Divine Matrix*
*The Divine Name* (with Jonathan Goldman)
*Fractal Time*
*The Gregg Braden Audio Collection\**
*Speaking the Lost Language of God*
*The Spontaneous Healing of Belief*
*Unleashing the Power of the God Code*

## DVD

*The Science of Miracles*

\*All of the above are available from Hay House
except items marked with an asterisk.
Please visit:
Hay House USA: www.hayhouse.com®
Hay House Australia: www.hayhouse.com.au
Hay House UK: www.hayhouse.co.uk
Hay House India: www.hayhouse.co.in

# *the* wisdom codes

### ancient words
### to rewire our brains
### and heal our hearts

## GREGG BRADEN

HAY HOUSE, INC.

Carlsbad, California • New York City
London • Sydney • New Delhi

Copyright © 2020 by Gregg Braden

*Published in the United States by:* Hay House, Inc.: www.hayhouse.com®
*Published in Australia by:* Hay House Australia Pty. Ltd.: www.hayhouse.com.au
*Published in the United Kingdom by:* Hay House UK, Ltd.: www.hayhouse.co.uk
*Published in India by:* Hay House Publishers India: www.hayhouse.co.in

*Cover design:* Barbara LeVan Fisher • *Interior design:* Bryn Starr Best

Grateful acknowledgment is made to the HeartMath Institute for permission to use their Quick Coherence® Technique.

Grateful acknowledgment is made for permission to reproduce excerpts from:

*Prayers of the Cosmos* by Neil Douglas-Klotz (San Francisco: HarperSanFrancisco, 1994).

*Rengetsu: Life and Poetry of Lotus Moon*, translated by John Stevens (Brattleboro, VT: Echo Point Press Books and Media, 2014).

*Hsin-Hsin Ming: Seng-ts'an Third Zen Patriarch* by Richard B. Clarke (Buffalo, NY: White Pine Press, 2011).

All rights reserved. No part of this book may be reproduced by any mechanical, photographic, or electronic process, or in the form of a phonographic recording; nor may it be stored in a retrieval system, transmitted, or otherwise be copied for public or private use—other than for "fair use" as brief quotations embodied in articles and reviews—without prior written permission of the publisher.

The author of this book does not dispense medical advice or prescribe the use of any technique as a form of treatment for physical, emotional, or medical problems without the advice of a physician, either directly or indirectly. The intent of the author is only to offer information of a general nature to help you in your quest for emotional, physical, and spiritual well-being. In the event you use any of the information in this book for yourself, the author and the publisher assume no responsibility for your actions.

**Library of Congress has cataloged the earlier edition as follows:**

Names: Braden, Gregg, author.
Title: The wisdom codes : ancient words to rewire our brains and heal our
  hearts / Gregg Braden.
Description: 1st edition. | Carlsbad, California : Hay House, Inc., 2020. |
Identifiers: LCCN 2020004046 | ISBN 9781401949341 (hardback) | ISBN
  9781401949358 (ebook)
Subjects: LCSH: Language and languages--Religious aspects. | Language and
  languages--Miscellanea. | Thought and thinking. | Sacred books--History
  and criticism.
Classification: LCC BL65.L2 B73 2020 | DDC 200--dc23
LC record available at https://lccn.loc.gov/2020004046

**Tradepaper ISBN:** 978-1-4019-6523-5
**E-book ISBN:** 978-1-4019-4935-8
**Audiobook ISBN:** 978-1-4019-5690-5

12  11  10  9  8  7  6  5  4
1st edition, May 2020
2nd edition, May 2021

Printed in the United States of America

SUSTAINABLE
FORESTRY
INITIATIVE

Certified Chain of Custody
Promoting Sustainable Forestry
www.forests.org
SFI-01268

SFI label applies to the text stock

# CONTENTS

*A single word has the power to influence
the expression of genes that regulate
physical and emotional stress.*

— ANDREW NEWBERG, M.D., NEUROSCIENTIST,
AND MARK ROBERT WALDMAN

*I know nothing in the world
that has as much power as a word.*

— EMILY DICKINSON, POET

# PREFACE

Almost universally we use words to comfort ourselves in times of need. From the Blessing Way prayer used by the Navajo of the American desert Southwest (*Diné* in their own tongue) to honor natural order in times of chaos to the Old Testament Priestly Blessing discovered on two tiny silver scrolls dating to nearly 3,000 years ago, world history is filled with examples of words that have soothed, comforted, and protected us. Individually and collectively, formally and informally, out loud and under our breath, through the ages, we humans have employed special words to help us navigate the difficult moments of life.

If we think of our creations as the expression of ideas that live within us, then our art, film, music, and writing take on a meaning of something more than simple entertainment. Such a relationship between our inner and outer worlds leads us to view our inspiration as consciousness informing itself— reminding us of our untapped possibilities and potential. From this perspective, the spiritual traditions of the past, and the words that preserve them, are living examples that reveal a timeless communication.

In writing *The Wisdom Codes*, I envisioned a collection of trusted words that we've historically turned to in times of need, distilled into an easy-to-read, quick-access, modern-day manual. This group of revered prayers, mantras, chants, and hymns is designed to provide reassurance, protection, and healing when life brings danger, hurt, unspeakable loss, and self-doubt to our doorstep. In such times, even the most well-meaning support of family and friends often falls short of finding its way into the dark void of our emotional abyss. In such times, all we may have is ourselves. And ultimately, that's all we need. Once I understood this simple truth, it made perfect sense that we already have the power to rewire our brains on demand, and in doing so, to choose—*to self-regulate*—the way we respond to life's extremes.

Through consciously applying the word codes of the past to the challenges we face in the moment, we benefit from the wisdom of ancient sages, healers, mystics, and prophets. In doing so, we're no longer victims. We are no longer defined by our circumstances but become masters of our destiny.

And this is the power of the *wisdom codes*. In their presence, we are changed. When we speak the words, either out loud or silently to ourselves, something shifts within us. And that "something" is where the power of words, chemistry, and neurons converge in a beautiful way. We associate the words of the codes with the meaning we give to the words. This association directs our brain cells (neurons) to connect in a precise way that harmonizes our biology with the energy of our emotions. Chemically, we are no longer the same person we were only moments or hours before. And it's that difference that opens the door to new ways of thinking, feeling, and acting when it comes to our losses, fears, and betrayals.

And while our changes may be subtle and perhaps will even go unnoticed by those with whom we share our lives, it's precisely these changes that gives us the wisdom, confidence, and power to awaken a deeper power within ourselves.

# INTRODUCTION

We think in words.

We speak in words.

In the silence of our minds, we hear the word-messages of our subconscious thoughts repeating at the dizzying rate of 60,000 to 80,000 times each day, according to scientific estimates. And now new evidence suggests that the power of our words extends far beyond what these statistics have revealed in the past. Recent studies confirm a theory that was first proposed early in the 20th century: that the words of our everyday language directly influence the way our brain "wires" itself when it comes to *how* we think, and even *what* we are capable of thinking about.

## THE DISCOVERY

The discovery of our word-brain relationship is not the product of well-coordinated research in a state-of-the-art laboratory searching for such a mystical-sounding link. Rather it's the result of an unexpected realization that emerged from an unplanned teaching assignment between 1937 and 1938. It was during this time that American linguist Benjamin Lee Whorf found himself substitute instructing a graduate-level class in Native American linguistics.

While filling in for a colleague who was on a year-long sabbatical, Whorf recognized a previously overlooked nuance in the language of the North American Hopi. Speakers of this language describe the events of everyday life without using—*or even referencing*—the experience of time. In other words, the Hopi language uses words that describe the present moment, and what's happening in the moment, with no words to directly describe the past or future.

It was this paradigm-altering use of language that led Whorf to the discovery that our words influence the way our neurons connect—a discovery that shattered the scientific beliefs of his day and remains controversial, as well as acclaimed, today.

## SPEAKING THE MOMENT

The indigenous experience of seeing lightning in the sky is a perfect illustration of Whorf's discovery. When the Hopi refer to lightning, their language describes it as a verb that's occurring, rather than a noun for something that exists. They say the equivalent of "It is lightning-ing," indicating that the lightning is in a *state of being*, rather than observing "the lightning" as a natural object.

In a similar way, when considering the ocean, rather than describing a single wave as the noun *the wave* or *a wave*, the Hopi see the wave as part of an all-inclusive system that is present, alive, and happening in the moment. Their thinking is reflected in the language that describes the experience, and they say, "The wave is wav-ing," just as a lightning bolt is "lightning-ing."

## THE WORDS OF A LIVING UNIVERSE

It's these word structures that Whorf believed were responsible for the harmonious way the Hopi think of themselves, structure their lives, and view their relationship to the cosmos. When considering the entirety of creation, for example, they see a living universe of connectivity that emerged long ago from a primal state of harmony. Within this system of oneness, the Hopi view cooperation between people and within nature as everyday expressions of a universal harmony that extends throughout the cosmos.

This life-affirming way of thinking stands in sharp contrast to the conventional scientific perspective that describes the universe as a "dead" system that emerged from a series of random and unbelievably fortunate cosmic events long ago. From this worldview of lucky biology, mainstream science attributes our origin, and continued existence, to the success of competition and what 19th-century naturalist Charles Darwin called *survival of the strongest*—a premise that the best science of the 21st century now tells us simply is not true. New discoveries in biology, as well as other life sciences, now reveal that cooperation, not competition, is the fundamental rule of nature.

## WORDS CAN CHANGE YOUR BRAIN

The implications of the word-life relationship are profound. It appears that the language we use—*the words we choose to describe ourselves and share our thoughts, feelings, emotions, and beliefs*—actually forms the framework for the unity or separation that we experience when we think and solve the problems of everyday life.

These proven word-brain relationships now have opened the door to an even deeper question: Is it possible that by choosing specific words to address the challenges in our lives, we could rewire our brains to discover new ways of solving our problems? In other words, can the conscious choice of words and word patterns help us actually to think and feel differently in times of crisis, trauma, loss, and need? The short answer is yes. The long answer is what the rest of this book is all about. As we'll see in the pages that follow, our ancestors held precisely this belief. And beyond simply acknowledging such a powerful bridge between words and biology, they applied their understanding as word codes in their times of need.

In the recent book *Words Can Change Your Brain*, physician Andrew Newberg, M.D., and co-author Mark Waldman echo Whorf's ideas and tell us precisely what the word-brain connection means. They describe this relationship clearly, stating: "A single word has the power to influence the expression of genes that regulate physical and emotional stress."

Additionally, Newberg and Waldman reveal a relationship between our words and our body that goes *beyond* the level of our genes, to impact our perception of reality itself. The phenomenon begins in the thalamus, a small gland near the center of the brain that relays sensory information to the areas of the brain that interpret, and then act upon, the signals to form our perceptions of the world. They write, "Over time the structure of your thalamus will also change in response to your conscious words, thoughts, and feelings, and we believe that the thalamic changes affect the way in which you perceive reality."

The discoveries they report on have added to a growing body of evidence revealing the power of words and how we may use them to help us in difficult moments.

## THE WISDOM CODES

Whorf's 20th-century discoveries and recent scientific revelations in the fields of neuroscience and biology are telling us the same story. They point to the same relationship. Our words influence the chemistry in our bodies, the neurons in our brains, and the way our neurons connect and "fire" to determine:

- *How* we think of ourselves and solve our problems
- *What* we are even capable of thinking about

These insights give new meaning to the chants, hymns, prayers, and mantras used in the traditions of the past. For thousands of years, precise words and ritual phrases have been spoken from father to son, mother to daughter, shaman to shaman, and healer to healer. And from the time of the earliest writings, these are the messages that were preserved for future generations in the sacred scripts and mysterious glyphs that have withstood the test of time. Today we find the legacy of our ancestors' efforts in some of the most remote, isolated, and hidden locations on earth—monasteries, temples, and tombs that stand as silent repositories of timeless wisdom. We also find this verbal legacy recorded in the sacred literature of the world's most-revered spiritual traditions.

Our ancestors preserved their secrets for the people living in their time, as well as for those living in a future they could only imagine—*for us*. They sensed that future generations would need the same emotional anchors and psychological strength to prevail in the struggles of war, climate extremes, and social chaos that they'd experienced in their day, which they suspected would return. From the ancient Sanskrit Vedas, believed to have originated over 7,000 years ago, to the Mahabharata, the teachings of the Buddha, the "lost" texts of the Judeo-Christian Bible, and the sacred mysteries of indigenous traditions, the power of the wisdom codes is available for us today if we understand what they mean and how to apply them to our circumstances.

## USING THIS BOOK

As many and varied as life's tests may seem to be at first glance, a closer look at the challenges that we face reveals a subtle relationship between our experience and our perceptions. The relationship is this: What we often perceive as separate issues are in reality different expressions of the same underlying issue. For example, while we commonly think of anger, jealousy, and criticism as separate issues to be dealt with one by one, each ultimately points to the same core issue: *unresolved fear.* By healing (resolving) our underlying fear, we dismantle the need for safety and the reasons why varied expressions of the same fear may be showing up in our lives.

Our ancestors understood these relationships. They also understood the power of the *cascade effect* in relationships—the healing of many emotions through the resolution of a single core fear. They shared what they discovered as the deep wisdom encoded in the sacred words that have survived the test of time.

With these ideas in mind, I've selected a core group of wisdom codes that address the issues that we most commonly face in life. These timeless codes are designed to bring us the greatest strength and the deepest healing, in the quickest way possible.

The first five parts of this book are each dedicated to one of the core issues that challenge us most in life: protection, fear, loss, strength, and love. I've included two additional parts that empower us through their understanding and use. Part Six features the *power codes* "I am" and "I will," and Part Seven features two parables to remind us of two healing truths about ourselves.

For easy and consistent access, each section is arranged in the following format:

- The **wisdom code, power code, or parable** itself: a direct quote from a text, scripture, or revered teaching from our past

- The **use** of the wisdom code: the intended experience that the code is designed to address

- The **source** of the wisdom code with a reference for where you can go to read it directly, or to discover a greater context for yourself

- **Discussion** of the wisdom code: its context, meaning, and how we can apply it in our lives

While this book may be read from cover to cover as a continuous narrative, it is also designed as a manual—a collection of wisdom to have at our fingertips for quick reference and emotional strength.

Through the ancient words of those who have experienced in their lives the same challenges of loss, fear, difficult choices, and deep hurts that you face today, you are bound to those ancestors by the common thread of timeless human experience. It's in these moments that the centuries between then and now dissolve, and the mastery of the past can become your mastery in the moment. Thank you for exploring the wisdom codes in the pages that follow.

Gregg Braden
Santa Fe, New Mexico

# HOW TO USE THE
# WISDOM CODES

In times of need, I invite you to open *The Wisdom Codes*, go to the table of contents, and then explore a section that calls to you or reflects the nature of a challenge that you are facing in the moment.

The steps that follow describe a time-tested sequence for you to apply the wisdom codes and power codes in your life, in the same way that served our ancestors in the past.

**Step 1. Familiarize yourself with the wisdom code you have selected by reading its source and background.** This powerful first step creates an opening that invites the words of the past to serve you in the present. For example, knowing that the same words that protected Moses 3,000 years ago during his perilous journey to receive the Ten Commandments on Mount Sinai are available today gives us a reason to believe that the protection he received in his day is available for us as well.

**Step 2. Shift your focus with the Quick Coherence Technique.** The simple steps of shifting your focus and your breathing, described in the box on the next page, awaken a network of specialized cells in your heart known as *sensory neurites*, which sets a sequence of hormonal and electrical signals in your body into motion and creates an emotional opening for you to embrace a new point of view.

Focusing our awareness in the heart is effective because while the brain typically perceives the world as filled with polarity, such as left/right, good/bad, success/failure, and so on, the heart does not. It is a nonpolar organ. When we embrace word codes from the unified perspective of our heart's intelligence, we give ourselves objectivity and a healthier way of seeing our challenge.

Many of the paradigm-altering discoveries regarding the human heart have been made by scientists at the Heart-Math Institute, a pioneering research organization dedicated to understanding the full potential of the human heart. By understanding the conditions of focus and breathing that create harmony in the body (a state known as *psychophysical coherence*), we can create those conditions to optimize the potential of the word codes in our lives. The technique to achieve this harmony is appropriately called the Quick Coherence Technique because it has been refined into two simple steps.

Individually, these steps send signals to the body that relieve stress and optimize our potential for healing. Combined, the technique creates a full-body harmony that we typically experience in life when we feel safe and have a sense of well-being.

## The Quick Coherence Technique

**Begin by shifting to a heart focus and breathe.** Shift your focus from your mind to the area of your heart, and begin to breathe a little slower than usual, as if your breath is coming from your heart. As you slow your breathing, you are sending a signal to your body in general, and your heart specifically, that you are in a place that is safe and it's okay to turn your attention inward.

This step can be a powerful, stand-alone technique unto itself when you're feeling overwhelmed by the day's events or simply desire to be more connected with yourself. It also lays the foundation for Step B as follows.

**Then, activate a positive feeling.** From your heart center, make a sincere attempt to experience a regenerative feeling, such as gratitude, appreciation, or care for someone or something in your life. The key in this step is to first create the feeling to the best of your ability, and then to surrender to the feeling, fully embracing it while allowing it to radiate from your heart to fill your body and permeate your entire being.

The following simple steps create the conditions in your body to optimize the harmony, and the coherence, between your heart and your brain.

*(Adapted by permission from the HeartMath Institute)*

**Step 3. Reread the wisdom code. From the perspective of heart/brain connection that you created in Step 2, reread the wisdom code that you've chosen, either silently or out loud.** Without judging the ancient and sometimes awkward grammar, poor sentence structure, or differences in translation, allow the wisdom and the intent of the message to permeate your entire being in the present moment. To the best of your ability, feel the intent as if you're speaking the code, prayer, hymn, or mantra directly from your heart. Ancient traditions, such as those of the monks in Tibet, typically speak their wisdom codes as they exhale their breath.

Continue speaking or breathing the lines of your wisdom code for a minimum of three minutes. Scientists have found that this is a minimal time for the body to lock in its responses to the emotional shifts that you are creating through the word codes.

**Step 4. Notice how your body feels. Your body will respond quickly to the changes you create in your awareness and your breathing. While these shifts may be subtle at first, they become more apparent as you become more attuned to the sensations.**

- Pay attention to your physical sensations: Do you feel anxious or calm? Nervous or relaxed?

- Pay attention to your emotions: Do you feel fearful or safe? Out of control or in control?

There are no correct or incorrect experiences. The key here is to notice the difference that has occurred since you began the word-code process and now.

You may repeat this process multiple times a day, including as the first thing you do to begin your day and the last thing you do before you go to sleep at night. As with any other skill, the more you practice creating coherence between your heart and your brain, the easier it becomes to do so. And with that ease, the more natural the experience begins to feel. With growing ease, you'll be able to sustain the heart/brain connection for longer periods of time.

While the scientific studies describe coherence, and why it works as it does, our ancestors didn't need the science to benefit from the harmony that coherence gave them in their lives. They discovered that the techniques of regulating their breath and creating a heart focus in times of need gave them the edge they needed to survive the extremes of their lives. If you're interested in the scientific details of heart/brain coherence, its discovery, and its applications, please refer to Chapters 1–2 in my 2014 book *Resilience from the Heart* (see Resources).

# THE WORDS
# ARE THE CODES

*Words can light fires in the minds of men.*
*Words can wring tears from the hardest hearts.*

—Patrick Rothfuss, writer

    It's been said that the best way to hide something of value is to keep it in plain sight. The ancient Pyramid Texts discovered in the temple complex of Saqqâra, Egypt, offer a beautiful example of this principle. The vast labyrinth of chambers holds a secret that's been plainly visible for over 4,000 years to all who had access to the underground complex. The passages carved under the Fifth Dynasty pyramid of Unas are covered from floor to ceiling with hieroglyphs that reveal an astonishing message.

## A MAP TO THE NEXT WORLD

Inscribed, etched, and carved into the walls are the instructions for how the human soul travels in death from the physical body into the next world of the afterlife. But the remarkably well-preserved inscriptions offer more than simply a manual for how to accomplish the journey. Beyond the alchemy of the transition itself, the texts acknowledge myriad emotions, such as worry, doubt, anxiety, and fear, that inevitably come with such a journey.

Following a typical human lifetime of complex and intimate relationships, difficult choices, and the sheer challenges of survival, at the time of death the soul naturally questions the decisions it's made over the course of its lifetime. And it's this personal life assessment that can lead to a sense of doubt when it comes to the soul's feelings of being worthy of the next world.

In the absence of someone physically present to offer comfort and reassurance to the transitioning soul of King Unas, the ancient scribes who put these messages on the walls enlisted a substitute principle that would have been well-known to initiates of all religious sects in Egypt at the time. The key to supporting the soul on its journey at death was to trigger a powerful shift in thinking *before* the time of death. It's this shift that would initiate the physical process that assured a successful journey to the afterlife for the soul.

The success of this predeath initiation hinged upon the texts in the burial chambers being identical to texts that the soul—in this case, the soul of King Unas—had already become familiar with before his death. This means that at the time of his death the king was *already* thinking about his journey to the afterlife. He was *already* prepared emotionally to accommodate the shift of energy for the transition he was about to make. His brain had *already* been wired to support the new experience. The hieroglyphs on the temple walls were the catalyst for a shift in thinking that King Unas had already embraced. The key here is that the hieroglyphs (pictorial words) were the codes that triggered the shifts.

## THE SECRET IN THE HIMALAYAS

Each day on the Tibetan plateau is both summer and winter—summer in the intensity of the direct, high-altitude sun, and winter as the sun disappears behind the jagged peaks of the Himalayas. I'd invited 40 others to join me on a journey that led us here, halfway around the world into one of the most remote, isolated, magnificent, and sacred places of knowledge remaining today: an ancient Tibetan monastery.

For 14 days we'd acclimated our bodies to altitudes of over 16,000 feet above sea level. We'd crossed an icy river in hand-hewn wooden barges and driven for hours with eyes peering at one another over the tops of the surgical masks that shielded us from the dust cloud that floated through the floorboards of our vintage Chinese bus.

Holding onto the seats around us, and even onto one another, we had braced ourselves and been jarred from the inside out as we crossed washed-away bridges and roadless desert just to be in this very place. But the beauty of the destination was well worth the price of the bumps and the dust. If the monasteries were easy to get to, thousands of people would have made the journey through the ages, and the wisdom preserved in these timeless shrines likely would have been lost to "progress." On this day I found myself sitting with my group on the cold stone floor of a windowless chapel, waiting for our first meeting with the ranking elder of this ancient temple.

## THE WORDS ARE THE CODES

I focused my attention directly into the eyes of the beautiful and ageless-looking man, draped in maroon robes, seated lotus style in front of me. He was the abbot of the monastery. Through our translator, I'd just asked him the same question that I'd asked each monk and nun we'd met throughout our pilgrimage. "When we see your prayers," I began, "what are you *doing* in your body? When we see you tone and chant mantras for fourteen to sixteen hours a day on the outside, what is happening to you on the inside?"

As the translator shared the abbot's reply, a powerful sensation rippled through my body and I knew that this was the reason that we'd come to this place. "You have never seen our prayers," he answered, "because a prayer cannot be seen." Adjusting the heavy wool robes beneath his feet, the abbot continued. "What you have seen is what we do to create the feeling in our bodies. *The feeling is the prayer, and the words create the feeling!*"

## THE WISDOM CODES

The clarity of the abbot's answer reflected the discoveries that had been reported in recent scientific journals. He was telling me that the *words* of the ancient chants are catalysts that elicit the feelings that change the body of the person that offers them. The words are the codes.

His message echoed ideas recorded in the ancient scriptures of the Gnostic and Christian traditions of the West over 2,000 years ago.

In early translations of the biblical book of John (chapter 16, verse 24), for example, we are instructed to empower our prayers through the words that invite us to *be* surrounded by the feeling that our prayer is already answered. "Ask without hidden motive and *be* surrounded by your answer. *Be* enveloped by what you desire so that your joy may be full."

Here we see that it's the *words* that ignite the emotion that empowers our prayers as the cascade of events that follow. When we allow ourselves to fully embrace what our spoken words mean on the deepest possible levels of awareness, they trigger the neurological and biological responses that reflect the intent of the codes.

The potential power of catalyzing such a biological chain reaction is clearly identified by the scribe Thomas in the lost gospel of which he is the namesake. It states that if we do this, we could say to a mountain, "Mountain, move away," and it would move away.

If the wisdom was that powerful in antiquity and worked consistently over a vast period of time in the past, then it must still be useful to us today! Using nearly identical language, the Tibetan abbot and the Gnostic gospel were describing the same principle.

For over 5,000 years, our most ancient and cherished spiritual traditions have recognized the relationship between the words we use and the way our brains function. They relied upon specific word patterns that they would recite—prayers, mantras, hymns, and chants—to provide them with inspiration, safety, comfort, and healing when they were faced with the inevitable challenges of everyday life. And although ancient indigenous people were not scientists by today's standards, they understood the effect of the word codes full well.

Though the times have changed, we're not so different from our ancestors in how we respond when life's tests arrive at our doorsteps. We still reel from the loss of our loved ones. We still ask for protection when we're afraid. We still seek guidance when we make difficult choices. And like our ancestors, we still can benefit from the wisdom codes they discovered in their day.

# PART ONE

# protection

*I don't know if what I'm afraid of is the state of the world.*
*Rather, I think what I'm afraid of is the state of*
*my attitude about the state of the world.*

— CRAIG D. LOUNSBROUGH,
THERAPIST AND LIFE COACH

B ecause all humankind shares certain fears, we have a universal sense that we sometimes need refuge and protection. Sometimes we feel a need to protect ourselves from forces that may be seen, such as an obvious physical threat. If we're protecting ourselves from an angry co-worker, for example, we take the steps we need to avoid or resolve the anger that's directed toward us. This is the kind of protection that's the easiest to identify, justify, and remedy.

But sometimes we feel the need to protect ourselves from forces that are not so obvious, because we can't see them. Unseen forces can be more difficult to remedy. These are the forces that our ancestors addressed through the use of wisdom codes that shift our perspective, and in turn, the chemistry of our bodies, to shield us when we feel the need for personal protection. The following wisdom codes for protection are taken from traditional prayers of the Christian, Buddhist, and Vedic traditions.

# wisdom code 1

## Psalm 91

WISDOM CODE 1: He that dwelleth in the secret place of the Most High shall abide under the shadow of the Almighty. I will say of the Lord, He is my refuge and my fortress: my God; in him will I trust.

USE: Protection. This code was created by the prophet Moses as he climbed Mount Sinai to shield him from unknown forces during his ascent. It's become a standard for protection that's use ranges from the challenges of everyday life to the safety of entire armies preparing for battle.

SOURCE: The Bible, King James Version, Psalms, chapter 91, verses 1–2

A mong the 39 books in the Old Testament of the Protestant Christian Bible, the book of Psalms is unique. The general theme of the 18 books that precede Psalms, and of the 20 that follow it, is that they primarily contain information, instructions, and commands directed *from* God *to* the people of the earth. This is where Psalms is different. It does just the opposite.

Rather than preserving divine revelations received *from* God, the 2,461 verses that make up the book of Psalms are hymns—songs of honor and adoration—designed to be offered *to* God. In other words, the psalms are prayers ready-made for situations that range from the general challenges of everyday life to specific prayers designed for families and communities in times of need.

Psalm 91, also known on occasion as the Prayer of Moses, the Prayer of Protection, and the Soldier's Prayer, is one of the most powerful examples of what I mean here.

*Note:* Due to differences in translation and the way the psalms are numbered, Psalm 91 in the King James Bible was Psalm 90 in the much earlier ancient Greek version of the Bible called the Septuagint, which predates it by approximately 1,700 years.

## PSALM 91

The ancient Hebrew Zohar, the foundational text of the mystical Kabbalah, describes how Psalm 91 protected the prophet Moses the second time he climbed to the top of Mount Sinai, which is when he received the Ten Commandments. The Zohar describes how Moses was enveloped during his ascent by a mysterious cloud of unknown substance of unknown origin. The cloud became so dense that he could no longer see ahead of him, nor could he be seen by those watching him from below the cloud. Moses did not know what was happening, what the cloud meant, or what to expect. He didn't know if he'd ever reunite with his family, friends, and followers again.

It's during this time of uncertainty and fear that Moses composed and recited Psalm 91 for his protection. For reasons that he attributed to the power of this prayer, Moses, in fact, was protected. He continued to climb until he reached the top of Mount Sinai where he received the stone tablets inscribed with instructions that have been the primary law for followers of the Jewish and Christian faiths for the last 3,000-plus years.

Although Moses's original prayer in its entirety consisted of 16 verses, it's often abbreviated to the first two verses that follow, for ease of use and when time is of the essence:

> *He that dwelleth in the secret place of the Most High shall abide under the shadow of the Almighty.*
>
> *I will say of the Lord, He is my refuge and my fortress: my God; in Him will I trust.*

A closer look at this prayer reveals that the source of the protection it provides comes from the deeper layers of meaning that may be known by those who understand the code.

## THE CODED NAMES OF GOD

While entire books have been dedicated to revealing the mystery of Moses's Prayer of Protection, in the following discussion I will focus upon the coded names for God that are found throughout the prayer and the protection that they provide us, starting with *Most High*.

## Coded Name 1: MOST HIGH

The first encoded name of God is *Most High*. In biblical Hebrew, this is typically translated from Aramaic (the original language of the scriptures) as *El Elyon*, meaning "God most high" or "God the highest," indicating that nothing can be greater or more powerful than the essence of the force represented in this name. This application of this word code is seen early in the Old Testament (Genesis 14:18–20): "Blessed be Abram by God *Most High*, Creator of heaven and earth. And blessed be God *Most High*, who delivered your enemies into your hand."

## Coded Name 2: ALMIGHTY

The second of God's hidden names is the word *Almighty* and is typically translated by Near Eastern scholars from Aramaic as *Shaddai* (meaning "Almighty") or *El Shaddai* (meaning "God Almighty"). This is one of the seven names of God that are substituted for God's actual name over 6,800 times in the Hebrew Bible. The other six names are *Ehyeh*, meaning "I will be"; *Tzevaot*, meaning "host"; *Elohim*, meaning "gods"; *El*, meaning "God"; and *Eloah*, also meaning "God."

## Coded Name 3: LORD

The third coded name is perhaps the most direct, mysterious, and powerful. It is the personal name of God: *Yahweh*. Following the initial revelation of his identity to Moses on Mount Sinai as "I Am," Moses asked for a clarification as to how he should address God when in his presence. The reply was the one-time revelation of God's personal name to the people of the earth. In Exodus 6:2–3, God stated to Moses in no uncertain terms, "I am Yahweh."

In the earliest records of the Hebrew Bible, before the writing of the authoritative, 6th-century Masoretic texts, God's personal name is clearly identified as Yahweh. Because Orthodox Jewish tradition holds this name so sacred, however, it is never to be written or spoken as a common word. For these reasons, God's personal name has been replaced approximately 6,800 times in the Hebrew Bible with alternative names, such as Adonai, Elohim, and Lord.

## Coded Name 4: GOD

The fourth coded name, God, is translated from the Hebrew *Elohim* and is the most common name used for God in the Old Testament. While there continues to be uncertainty, and mystery, as to the precise translation of this word, it is typically associated with God the Creator.

The first insights into the nature of this mysterious word are found in Genesis 1:1, where the first sentence states: "In the beginning God created the heaven and the earth." In this reference, God is referred to in the singular as the Creator. Later, in Genesis 1:27, however, we are given a deeper sense of the power of this creation.

Genesis 1:27 begins: "So God created man in *his* own image, in the image of God created he him," indicating humankind is a reflection of a singular essence. Yet in the second part of the same sentence, the description of this primal act of creation expands: "Male and female created he *them*," a reference that is dual rather than singular. (The italics are mine.) In this way, we are shown the all-inclusive power of the Creator as both singular and plural.

## The Soldier's Prayer

In addition to offering a source of personal protection, since the time of its origin, Psalms 91 has also been used as a prayer of protection by entire armies as they prepare themselves for battle. During World War I, for example, it was common for military units to be given the assignment of memorizing the Soldier's Prayer the night before battle. In doing so, Moses's Prayer of Protection occupied their hearts and minds, preparing them for the hand-to-hand combat they were about to face on the battlefields of Europe.

As mentioned previously, while the first two verses are often recited as a brief prayer of protection, the entire prayer can be, and often is, used as well. Following is the complete version of Psalm 91—with the various names of God in the individual lines highlighted for your convenience.

*He that dwelleth in the secret place of the Most High shall abide under the shadow of the Almighty.*

*I will say of the Lord, He is my refuge and my fortress: my God; in him will I trust.*

*Surely he shall deliver thee from the snare of the fowler, and from the noisome pestilence.*

*He shall cover thee with his feathers, and under his wings shalt thou trust: his truth shall be thy shield and buckler.*

*Thou shalt not be afraid for the terror by night; nor for the arrow that flieth by day;*

*Nor for the pestilence that walketh in darkness; nor for the destruction that wasteth at noonday.*

*A thousand shall fall at thy side, and ten thousand at thy right hand; but it shall not come nigh thee.*

*Only with thine eyes shalt thou behold and see the reward of the wicked.*

*Because thou hast made the Lord, which is my refuge, even the Most High, thy habitation;*

*There shall no evil befall thee, neither shall any plague come nigh thy dwelling.*

*For he shall give his angels charge over thee, to keep thee in all thy ways.*

*They shall bear thee up in their hands, lest thou dash thy foot against a stone.*

*Thou shalt tread upon the lion and adder: the young lion and the dragon shalt thou trample under feet.*

*Because he hath set his love upon me, therefore will I deliver him: I will set him on high, because he hath known my name.*

*He shall call upon me, and I will answer him: I will be with him in trouble; I will deliver him, and honor him.*

*With long life will I satisfy him, and show him my salvation.*

## HOW TO USE WISDOM CODE 1

The power of wisdom codes comes from their repetition and doing so in the affirmative. This imprints a code on the subconscious mind. When we create heart/brain harmony, as described in "How to Use the Wisdom Codes" (see page xix), we open a "hotline" to communicate directly with the subconscious mind.

From a place of heart/brain harmony, recite this code line by line, either silently in your mind or out loud, until you feel an increased sense of trust and certainty that you are not alone. The key is to embrace this code with a focus of awareness, breath, and feeling in the heart rather than the mind.

- *He that dwelleth in the secret place of the Most High shall abide under the shadow of the Almighty.*

- *I will say of the Lord, He is my refuge and my fortress: my God; in Him will I trust.*

11

# Notes

_____

_____

_____

_____

_____

_____

_____

_____

_____

_____

_____

_____

_____

# wisdom code 2

## Buddhist Prayer of Refuge

WISDOM CODE 2: In the Buddha, the Dharma, and the Sangha, I take refuge until I attain enlightenment.

USE: Protection. This code addresses the need for personal protection at a spiritual level for a specific period.

SOURCE: Abbreviated form of the traditional Tibetan Buddhist Prayer of Refuge. The full text is included in the discussion that follows.

The Buddhist Prayer of Refuge has uncertain origins. While the great yogi Atiśa (Atiśa Dīpamkara Śrījñāna) is often thought to be the author, there remains uncertainty and controversy as to whether he personally created the prayer or was so instrumental in spreading the teachings that it is attributed to him. As a master teacher of the Buddhist traditions, Atiśa organized and distilled the essence of Buddha's 84,000 teachings into a single, seminal text that is still used today. In his classic text *Lamp for the Path to Enlightenment*, Atiśa describes the practices that comprise the Buddhist Prayer of Refuge.

Wisdom Code 2 is known by names that include the Prayer of Refuge, the Instruction on Refuge, Atiśa's Refuge Prayer, and more commonly, the Prayer of the Three Jewels. In the Tibetan tradition, the prayer is called *kyamdro*, which is understood to be an instruction to take refuge in the three foundational elements, or jewels, of Buddhism: the Buddha (the teachings of the enlightened being who discovered the path), the Dharma (the eternal truth of reality), and the Sangha (the community of other Buddhists—traditionally nuns, monks, and supplicants), described in the following paragraphs.

## ANATOMY OF TIBETAN BUDDHIST PROTECTION

The chemical codes of human life, our DNA strands, are typically simplified by using four letters of the alphabet—C, T, A, G—as a shorthand representing the four proteins that make life possible: cytosine, thymine, adenine, and guanine. While some proteins contain as many as hundreds of underlying amino acids, by using different combinations of the shorthand, it becomes possible to read, write, and describe even the most complex proteins quickly and easily. The Buddhist Prayer of Refuge works in a very similar way.

While the prayer itself contains many layers of depth and meaning, the essence of the prayer is represented by only three brief verses. And just as the simple letters C, T, A, and G represent a deeper meaning for the DNA codes, each verse of Wisdom Code 2 represents a deeper understanding of ourselves and the experiences of our lives. Following is a brief anatomy of this prayer, describing the meaning of *refuge* itself, and four underlying principles that give us varying degrees of refuge in our lives.

## THE MEANING OF *REFUGE*

The traditional Buddhist texts describe different kinds and varying degrees of refuge that we may seek over the course of our lives. With respect to Wisdom Code 2, the word *refuge* can initially mean protection from suffering by turning to ways of thinking and living that reflect the teachings of the Buddha. This kind of refuge is described as taking the form of three "objects" or principles: the Buddha, the Dharma, and the Supreme Assembly, or Sangha. Following is a brief description of each principle and what it means in our lives.

### Principle 1. Refuge in the Buddha

The first object of refuge is the path of the Buddha, or Buddhism itself. To "take refuge in the Buddha" is to commit to a path of conscious thought and mindful action designed to lead to a greater state of awareness of ourselves, as well as our relationship to the world. This path requires a commitment to a deeper relationship between us and the enlightenment that Buddha tells us is possible in our lives.

## Principle 2. Refuge in the Dharma

The second object of refuge is the Dharma. Within the context of Buddha's Prayer of Protection, this refuge is found in the writings (Buddhist scriptures) that harmonize the unsettled and fearful emotions of the mind. Shifting our attention from the chaotic matters of the world to the harmony that's reflected in nature and the human body frees us from fear and suffering.

## Principle 3. Refuge in the Sangha

The third object of refuge is the Sangha. This is a reference to spending time in the company of *Bodhisattvas*, beings who have achieved an advanced state of consciousness. These are compassionate beings who, although they have already reached a state of enlightenment, choose to remain in the unenlightened realm of everyday life on earth to ease the suffering of those who have not yet achieved the same state.

## Principle 4: Pray for an Unlimited Duration

There is a fourth principle that brings this code to completion. This is the last and final portion of the recitation that specifies the duration of the refuge and protection that the person using the code is striving for. This parameter is simply stated: "Until I attain enlightenment." In the Mahayana sect of Buddhism, this state of enlightenment is clearly described. It is the successful realization of the Bodhisattva consciousness. Taken literally, the conclusion of Wisdom Code 2 tells us that the refuge and protection we're asking for is to be sustained until we've reached enlightenment and become a

Bodhisattva. The vow that combines these four principles is the source of the code's power.

The English translation of this timeless wisdom code is spoken as follows:

> *In the Buddha, the Dharma, and the Sangha, I take*
> *refuge until I attain enlightenment.*

In the Sanskrit language that was the code's origin, each fragment of the wisdom code begins with the word *namo*, meaning "homage" or "reverence." It is spoken like this:

> *Namo Buddhaya;*

> *Namo Dharmaya;*

> *Namo Sanghaya.*

## HOW TO USE WISDOM CODE 2

The power of wisdom codes comes from their repetition and doing so in the affirmative. This imprints a code on the subconscious mind. When we create heart/brain harmony, as described in "How to Use the Wisdom Codes" (see page xix), we open a "hotline" to communicate directly with the subconscious mind.

From a place of heart/brain harmony, recite the version that you are most drawn to, silently or out loud—line by line—until you feel an increased sense of trust and certainty that you are not alone. The key is to embrace this code with a focus of awareness, breath, and feeling in the heart rather than the mind.

### English Translation of the Ancient Sanskrit

*In the Buddha, the Dharma, and the Sangha, I take refuge until I attain enlightenment.*

### Original Words in Ancient Sanskrit

*Namo Buddhaya;*

*Namo Dharmaya;*

*Namo Sanghaya.*

# Notes

_____

_____

_____

_____

_____

_____

_____

_____

_____

_____

_____

_____

_____

_____

# Notes

_____

_____

_____

_____

_____

_____

_____

_____

_____

_____

_____

_____

_____

# wisdom code 3

## The Lord's Prayer

WISDOM CODE 3: Our Father in heaven, hallowed be thy name; thy kingdom come; thy will be done; as in heaven so on earth.

USE: This code addresses the need for personal protection on both a physical and a spiritual level.

SOURCE: This portion of the Lord's Prayer is translated from the original Syriac dialect of an ancient Aramaic gospel. It is a shortened, stand-alone version of the longer original prayer that appears in Matthew, chapter 6, verses 9–13, and in a briefer version in Luke, chapter 11, verses 2–4.

The Lord's Prayer, also on occasion known as the Our Father Prayer, is arguably the best known and most widely used ancient word code in the Christian tradition. As recognized as it is, however, there remains controversy among scholars as to (1) where the words of the prayer originated and (2) how much liberty has been taken with the words in the various translations over the centuries.

## THE MYSTERIOUS SOURCE OF THE LORD'S PRAYER:
### The Lost Gospel Q

Biblical scholars suspect that the Lord's Prayer originated in one of two possible places in the New Testament of the Christian Bible.

The longer form of the prayer comes from the book of Matthew. It is part of Jesus's historic teaching known as the Sermon on the Mount and is recorded in chapter 6, verses 9–13 of this traditional gospel.

A briefer form of the prayer is derived from another teaching that Jesus offered his disciples that is not the Sermon on the Mount. This version is described in Luke, chapter 11, verses 2–4.

The controversy about its origins stems from the fact that the Lord's Prayer *is not* recorded in what's considered to be one of the most reliable records of historic events that occurred in Jesus's day: the book of Mark. The question is why it would be noted in the books of Matthew and Luke, yet would be curiously absent in Mark? The answer has emerged with the discovery of a hidden, yet revered, biblical gospel discovered only recently, in the late 20th century: the Lost Gospel of Quelle. *Quelle* means "source" in German. Scholars typically shorten the name to the Gospel Q or simply Q.

The Gospel Q did not appear suddenly and obviously like the "lost" Gospel of Thomas, which was discovered intact by two brothers in a sealed jar near the Egyptian village of Nag Hammadi in 1945, for example; nor like the Dead Sea Scrolls, which were discovered intact in the Qumran caves of the Judean desert between the late 1940s and the early 1950s. In fact, it does not exist today as a stand-alone text. Rather, this "lost" gospel emerged slowly over a period, *emerging from within the paragraphs and pages* of already existing texts. It was only through the meticulous and scholarly work of text comparison among various translations of different gospels that Gospel Q was eventually recognized by 20th-century biblical scholars.

I'm describing Gospel Q here because it holds the key to the protective power of Wisdom Code 3. The version of the Lord's Prayer in Gospel Q represents its oldest version, in which are preserved what are believed to be the original words that Jesus shared with his followers. It's for this reason that I have chosen the English translation closest to the original words of Jesus's time as possible, which was prepared by George M. Lamsa in the early 20th century.

## JESUS'S ORIGINAL WORDS

The traditional language used in regions of Nazareth and Capernaum, where Jesus lived and taught, was Aramaic. This language first emerged in the Holy Land roughly 3,000 years ago and is still used today in some Jewish, Mandaean, and Christian communities. Scholars generally agree that Jesus spoke the Lord's Prayer in this ancient language, and that it was recorded in written Aramaic as well. Supporting evidence for this assumption is found in ancient translations of New Testament manuscripts.

These ancient records confirm that it is Aramaic, not Hebrew, that would have been used by Jesus when he shared his public sermons and teachings. For example, the oldest-known versions of the New Testament, which were discovered in Egypt's Nag Hammadi Library, show that the names by which Jesus referred to his disciples were Aramaic. The name *Cephas*, for example, is Aramaic for "Peter," and *Thomas* is Aramaic for "twin." Determining the language used during Jesus's time is important because the precise language holds the key to the words, and the power, of the Lord's Prayer.

While scholars *do* agree that Aramaic was the language of Jesus's day, another question (one whose answer they do *not* agree on) is *which dialect* of Aramaic was used when Jesus revealed the Lord's Prayer to his disciples. While the scholarly arguments are beyond the scope of what I can describe in these pages, I've chosen to focus on what appears to be the most likely answer, based upon the oldest records of the New Testament—manuscripts written in a form of Aramaic known as *ancient Syriac*. According to scholar and author Stephen Andrew Missick, "This form of Aramaic is very similar to, but not exactly identical with, the Aramaic spoken by Jesus." I'm sharing this level of detail because the English translation of the Syriac Lord's Prayer is the first version that we'll explore as Wisdom Code 3.

## THE UNIVERSAL CODE

The structure of the Lord's Prayer is eloquent. It is sophisticated and simple. Perhaps it's not a coincidence that the format of this ancient word code follows precisely the same format used by modern computer systems today. Regardless of the size and complexity of a modern-day computer, from a microcomputer programmed with 3 lines of software to a room-sized supercomputer running from 3 million lines of software, the format of the language that runs the machines is the same. It uses the same general structure composed of three simple functions. These are the parts of this universal template:

1. A declaration statement.

2. A function statement.

3. A completion (or resolution) statement.

From the software that sends humans into space and brings them safely home again to the programs that distribute electricity across the power grids of the world, the same universal structure applies. And perhaps it's precisely because this format appears to reflect universal principles for the way information flows in the world that this format applies to the code of the Lord's Prayer, as well.

The first phrase of the code is the declaration statement. These words set the stage and declare to the universe what is about to occur. They are followed by the function statements that describe what the prayer is meant to accomplish (several things). These in turn are followed by the completion statement that ends the prayer.

Biblical scholars typically refer to the multipart function statement as the speaker's "petitions." Scholars have identified seven petitions in the full version of the Lord's Prayer, and three petitions in the abbreviated version.

## SPEAKING THE LORD'S PRAYER IN ENGLISH

For the purposes of teaching about the protective power of Wisdom Code 3, I'll begin with an abbreviated form of the Lord's Prayer excerpted from the Syriac translation described previously. While it is brief, this form of the prayer is whole and complete unto itself and is often used in times of chaos or when danger is imminent, and time is short. I've organized the prayer into its three parts and offer a brief explanation of each component.

## The Introduction

*Our Father in heaven.*

The introduction is the declaration statement. It creates conditions and paves the way for the success of the code that follows.

## The First Petition

*Hallowed be thy name.*

The word *hallowed* appears to be the best translation of the ancient Syriac script into modern English. It means to set God's name apart from all other words as special, holy, and sacred rather than a common word.

## The Second Petition

*Thy kingdom come.*

In this context, *kingdom* is the essence of God. Here the use of the word *thy* is not asking for God's kingdom to arrive on earth; rather, it is declaring that God's essence is present in all things and experiences.

## The Third Petition

*Thy will be done.*

In this context, the phrase *thy will* is referring to the stated parameters that God has identified in previous teachings, such as in the eight beatitudes specified in Jesus's teaching known as the *Sermon on the Mount*. Once again, the word *thy* is not asking, but is declaring that God's will is already present in all things and experiences.

## The Completion

*As in heaven so on earth.*

This phrase provides closure for this first part of the code. It states that the earth is a mirror of the heavenly conditions identified in the first, second, and third petitions.

Even in this abbreviated form, the Lord's Prayer reflects the complete structure of the universal code described previously. And it's for this reason that this revered wisdom code is seen as a template—as the prayer of prayers—in the Christian tradition. The second and third petitions respectively—*Thy kingdom come / thy will be done*—are the portions of Wisdom Code 3 that provide the protection that is being invoked. The intent here is clear and simple: In the context of God's kingdom, and in the presence of God's will, the divine nature described in these statements replaces any darkness and danger that may confront us.

## Missing: The Kingdom, Power, and Glory?

In some translations of the Bible, such as the Revised Standard Version, we see the portion of the Lord's Prayer that is commonly used to complete the prayer—*For thine is the kingdom, the power, and the glory forever*—which is not present in the original. This familiar way of completing the prayer as it is often spoken in churches today is known as the *Byzantine doxology*, or simply the *doxology*.

The doxology clearly is *not* a part of the original prayer as it's recorded in the oldest version of the book of Matthew. Rather it appears later for the first time in the Didache, a secondary biblical text written after Jesus's time, in the first century of the common era.

## Speaking the Lord's Prayer Using the Aramaic Words

In recent times, the Aramaic words for the Lord's Prayer have been brought to mainstream attention through the writing of renowned scholar of religious studies Neil Douglas-Klotz, Ph.D. Because there are no precise word-for-word correspondences between Aramaic and English, the original language lends itself to alternate interpretations. In 1990, Klotz released *Prayers of the Cosmos*, a short book that included the original Aramaic text of selected biblical texts that include the Lord's Prayer along with multiple possible translations and reinterpretations.

Since the time of its release, individuals and families, as well as small study groups and large theaters of people, have regularly used the following beloved translation to speak, honor, and reap the benefits of this powerful prayer. For those who would like to experience the sound and feeling of the actual words spoken by Jesus, I'm including Douglas-Klotz's phrase-by-phrase breakdown, as well as an approximate translation of the Lord's Prayer.

Note: If you'd like to recite this prayer using the original Aramaic words and pronunciation, a tutorial for the words is available online (see Resources).

| Aramaic Words | Approximate English Translation |
|---|---|
| *Abwoon d'bwashmaya* | *O Birther! Father-Mother of the Cosmos / you create all that moves in light.* |
| *Nethqadash shmakh* | *Focus your light within us— make it useful: as the rays of a beacon show the way.* |
| *Teytey malkuthakh* | *Create your reign of unity now—through our fiery hearts and willing hands.* |
| *Nehwey tzevyanach aykanna d'bwashmaya aph b'arha* | *Your one desire then acts with ours, as in all light so in all forms.* |
| *Hawvlan lachma d'sunqanan yaomana* | *Grant what we need each day in bread and insight; subsistence for the call of growing life.* |
| *Washboqlan khaubayn (wakhtahayn) aykana daph khnan shbwoqan l'khayyabayn* | *Loose the cords of mistakes binding us, as we release the strands we hold of others' guilt.* |
| *Wela tahlan l'nesyuna* | *Don't let us enter forgetfulness* |
| *Ela patzan min bisha.* | *But break the hold of unripeness* |
| *Metol dilakhie malkutha wahayla wateshbukhta l'ahlam almin* | *From you is born all ruling will, the power and the life to do, the song that beautifies all, from age to age it renews.* |
| *Ameyn* | *Truly—power to these statements—may they be the source from which all my actions grow. Sealed in trust and faith. Amen.* |

## HOW TO USE WISDOM CODE 3

In the previous sections, I've identified the first three petitions of the Lord's Prayer that may be used as a prayer of protection, as well as the full version of the prayer in the original Aramaic. For convenience, on these pages I'll share the original version again, along with the common English translation.

The power of wisdom codes comes from their repetition and doing so in the affirmative. This imprints a code on the subconscious mind. When we create heart/brain harmony, as described in "How to Use the Wisdom Codes" (see page xix), we open a "hotline" to communicate directly with the subconscious mind.

From a place of heart/brain harmony, recite the version that you are most drawn to, silently or out loud—line by line—until you feel an increased sense of trust and certainty that you are not alone. The key is to embrace this code with a focus of awareness, breath, and feeling in the heart rather than the mind.

### Common English Translation of the Ancient Aramaic

- *Our Father in heaven, hallowed be thy name;*
- *Thy kingdom come;*
- *Thy will be done;*
- *As in heaven so on earth.*
- *Give us bread for our needs from day to day;*
- *And forgive us our offences as we have forgiven our offenders.*
- *And do not let us enter into temptation;*
- *But deliver us from evil.*

## Original Words in Ancient Aramaic

- *Abwoon d'bwashmaya;*
- *Nethqadash shmakh;*
- *TeyTey malkuthakh;*
- *Nehwey tzevyanach aykanna d'bwashmaya aph b'arha;*
- *Hawvlan lachma d'sunqanan yaomana;*
- *Washboqlan khaubayn (wakhtahayn) aykana daph khnan shbwoqan l'khayyabayn;*
- *Wela tahlan l'nesyuna;*
- *Ela patzan min bisha;*
- *Metol dilakhie malkutha wahayla wateshbukhta l'ahlam almin;*
- *Ameyn.*

# Notes

_____

_____

_____

_____

_____

_____

_____

_____

_____

_____

_____

_____

_____

# wisdom code 4

## Gayatri Mantra

WISDOM CODE 4: Brahma, the manifestation of spiritual energy, destroyer of sufferings, embodiment of happiness, bright like sun, destroyer of sins, divine, intellect who may inspire!

USE: This mantra, which is known as the Gayatri Mantra, addresses personal protection as well as the need to clear personal obstacles.

SOURCE: The Rig Veda, mandala (book) 3, hymn 62, verse 10

The Vedic Prayer of Refuge known as the Gayatri Mantra or the Great Mantra is so revered in the Hindu tradition that it's often referred to as the *Mother of the Vedas*. The original source of the Gayatri Mantra is the most ancient of the Vedic texts, the Rig Veda, mandala 3, hymn 62, verse 10. As one of the most widely used Vedic mantras, it's not surprising that the Gayatri Mantra has a long and complex past. Its 3,000-plus-year history includes multiple translations that reflect the varied interpretations of the translators throughout time.

For the purpose of this discussion, I'll begin with a generalized view of the mantra to give a sense of what it is and how it is stated. The following interpretation is from Hindu scholar Swami Vivekananda (1863–1902), and it is followed by a more in-depth translation of the original Sanskrit words. In the word-by-word translation, we'll discover why the Gayatri Mantra has been, and continues to be, a timeless code of refuge and protection in both the Hindu and Buddhist traditions.

Because there is no direct correspondence between the words of Sanskrit and those of the English language, any translation of the Gayatri Mantra is only an approximation of the original language and intent. With this in mind, Swami Vivekananda's interpretation of the mantra's general meaning is as follows:

> *We meditate on the glory of that Being who has produced this universe. May He enlighten our minds.*

This is a 20th-century translation of the same mantra from Hindu scholar Shri Gyan Rajhans, also accepted by modern yoga and Vedic scholars:

*O thou existence Absolute, Creator of the three dimensions, we contemplate upon thy divine light. May He stimulate our intellect and bestow upon us true knowledge.*

As different as these general interpretations are, both share a common meaning and intent, illustrating why the Gayatri Mantra is often used as a source of protection. Both translations of the mantra close with an invitation for divinity and divine knowledge to become part of our everyday lives. It's believed that through the enlightenment of the human mind, the thinking that makes anger and hostility possible will be cleansed from all involved—both the user of the mantra and those who may be threatening the user.

The Gayatri Mantra is used as a source of inner strength and power. In addition to protection, it is believed to endow us with a host of other benefits, among them a stronger mind (specifically enhanced concentration) and improved breathing and health.

## THE SANSKRIT CODE

Although the origin of the Gayatri Mantra circa 1800 B.C.E. predates the biblical gospels by over a millennium, it should come as no surprise that it follows the same template for prayer that we see in the Lord's Prayer. As detailed in Wisdom Code 3, this template reflects universal principles of information flow and utilizes the three parts identified previously as a template: a declaration, a function statement (or several), and a completion statement.

With these relationships in mind, below I share a possible translation of the original mantra, accompanied by the meaning of each word. This particular translation is the work of Hindu scholar Kumud Ajmani, Ph.D. For continuity, I'll also illustrate the relationship of these words within the context of the universal prayer template.

## Declaration

*Aum*

**Meaning:** God's ultimate name.

*Bhur Bhuvah Swaha*

**Meaning:** These words express the inherent qualities that exist as God. *Bhur* is existence. *Bhuvah* illustrates God's consciousness. *Swaha* tells us God is inherent in all things.

## Function Statement 1

*Tat Savitur Varenyam*

**Meaning:** Within the context of the Gayatri, this means that the user is selflessly directing praise to God. The word *tat* means "that," and in the Gayatri indicates that the praises are being directed to God. *Savitur* is a name for God as the source of all things, as well as God's blessings for humankind. *Varenyam* means "who is eligible/worthy" of receiving God's blessings.

## Function Statement 2

*Bhargo Devasya Dhimahi.*

**Meaning:** The three words of this statement further describe the qualities of God from a functional perspective. *Bhargo* describes the light that is God's love. *Devasya* is derived from the Sanskrit word *deva*, and illustrates the many facets of God's attributes, without which nothing can exist. *Dhimahi* means to place our focus on God.

## Completion Statement

*Dhiyo Yo Nah Prachodayat!*

**Meaning:** *Dhiyo* means "intellect" and is used in this mantra to ask God to direct our abilities and use of our intellect. *Yo* means "who" and reminds us that our prayer is for God alone. *Nah* means "ours" and signifies that our mantra is for all people in addition to ourselves. *Prachodayat* completes the mantra and signifies that the entire mantra is a request to God as we seek safety, peace, and happiness.

The Gayatri Mantra continues to cross the traditional boundaries of religion and spirituality and remains one of the most popular mantras used in the world today. Among the reasons for its popularity are the many and varied applications that lend themselves to the mantra. These include the protection that results from clearing of both physical and emotional obstacles that may appear along our path as we seek the deeper wisdom of spiritual growth.

## HOW TO USE WISDOM CODE 4

The power of wisdom codes comes from their repetition and doing so in the affirmative. This imprints a code on the subconscious mind. When we create heart/brain harmony, as described in "How to Use the Wisdom Codes" (see page xix), we open a "hotline" to communicate directly with the subconscious mind.

From a place of heart/brain harmony, recite the version that you are most drawn to, silently or out loud—line by line—until you feel an increased sense of trust and certainty that you are not alone. The key is to embrace this code with a focus of awareness, breath, and feeling in the heart rather than the mind.

### English Translation

*Brahma, the manifestation of spiritual energy; destroyer of sufferings; embodiment of happiness; bright like sun; destroyer of sins, divine; intellect who may inspire!*

## Sanskrit Words

- *Aum*
- *Bhur Bhuvah Swaha;*
- *Tat Savitur Varenyam;*
- *Bhargo Devasya Dhimahi;*
- *Dhiyo Yo Nah Prachodayat!*

# Notes

_____

_____

_____

_____

_____

_____

_____

_____

_____

_____

_____

_____

_____

_____

# PART TWO

# fear

*Only to the extent that we expose ourselves over and over to annihilation can that which is indestructible be found in us.*

— PEMA CHÖDRÖN, TIBETAN BUDDHIST NUN

We all experience fear. It's one of six emotions that scientists recognize as universal in all human populations. (The others are sadness, happiness, anger, surprise, and disgust.) In addition to being one of our universally shared experiences, fear also is one of the most mysterious. The reasons: fear appears in different ways, we experience it for different reasons, and it means different things to different people.

Fear can sometimes show up in our lives as symptoms that seem so far removed from the root cause of the fear that we don't immediately recognize the connection. Emotional experiences such as chronic anxiety, worry, and depression, as well as physical symptoms ranging from skin rashes, colds, and allergies to hypertension and dysfunction of the organs that we subconsciously associate with unresolved trauma, are examples of the myriad of signals that can reveal an underlying fear.

The pioneering work of Candace Pert, Ph.D., and her revolutionary book *Molecules of Emotion*, paved the way for the scientific foundation to understand how the chemical signals of our unresolved fears—known as fear-related *neuropeptides*—can be stored indefinitely in the tissues, glands, and organs of the body until our fear response has been resolved and the chemicals can be metabolized.

Behavioral scientists tell us that unsourced, seemingly unexplained experiences of fear are ultimately expressions of a single primal, typically subconscious fear: *the fear of annihilation and nonexistence.*

Fear of annihilation can be triggered by seemingly unrelated everyday experiences. Or more precisely, by our *perception* of everyday experiences. It's possible that our fear of nonexistence may be universal because we share the uncertainty of the human condition. One of the great ironies of the modern age is that, in spite of our grand technological achievements, we've yet to answer with scientific certainty the most basic questions of our existence: *Who are we? Where do we come from? Where do we go when we die?*

## SUBCONSCIOUS FEAR

Sometimes our fears are logical, rational, and make perfect sense. The impulse to jump backward when we see a spider dangling from a web in our living room or the queasy feeling in the pit of our stomach as we stare from a high-rise hotel balcony to the city street 20 stories below are natural responses. In these examples, the trigger for anxiety or trepidation is real; it's tangible and clearly present. Sometimes, however, the sources of our fears are not so obvious. They come from something that's hidden, subconscious, forgotten.

Scientists have demonstrated that most of our emotions, as well as the bulk of our daily actions, decisions, and behaviors, originate from a part of our brain that is not conscious: the subconscious mind that is responsible for 95 percent of our daily activities. Our fears are among those subconscious emotions. An example of a subconscious fear is commonly expressed by adults who grew up in alcoholic families: the fear of not being heard.

Within the context of alcoholic dysfunction, children and spouses frequently report feelings of being ignored, criticized, and discounted. If the family member is not anchored in a strong sense of self, with healthy self-esteem and a strong soul identity, it's easy for them to become lost and succumb to the feelings they experience. In the absence of a clear identity, they may believe the demeaning views that they experience in their unhealthy environment.

The danger is that the subconscious mind can easily associate criticism and lack of acknowledgment with a sense of invisibility and nonexistence. And while the defense mechanisms of outward anger or inner retreat may allow us to survive the moment, the unresolved nature of the resulting hurt or trauma may linger long after the moment of the experience. It's these unresolved traumas that "light up" as the symptoms that ultimately lead us to the source of our experience. *The key here is that as different as the expressions of our fears may appear to be, they actually stem from one of, or a combination of, three universal fears: the fear of abandonment, the fear of not being worthy of living, and the fear of annihilation.*

The controversy continues in academic circles as to whether these universal fears are learned, instinctual, or somehow passed through genetics from parent to child. While the debate continues with no end in sight, the words that give us comfort in the presence of our deepest and sometimes unknown fears have been acknowledged and understood for hundreds of years.

In his first inaugural address to the nation, U.S. President Franklin D. Roosevelt famously said: "The only thing we have to fear is fear itself." I think there's a lot of truth to this statement. With this idea in mind, I've chosen wisdom codes in this section that have given comfort and reassurance in times of fear for thousands of years.

## UNIVERSAL REMINDERS

When something is true, it's common to see that "something" appearing in many places and in many forms simply because it is universal. The wisdom codes in this section have been used by initiates, mystics, and prophets from around the world since the long-ago past to remind us of precisely such a truth: that something within us is eternal. There is a part of us that cannot be destroyed and will never disappear into nothing. And it's in this reminder of our enduring essence that the four wisdom codes in Part Two give us refuge from our fear of absolute annihilation.

The best science of the modern world supports this mystical view of our eternal nature, both mathematically and philosophically. For example, the law of conservation of energy, a fundamental principle of physics first described by Julius Robert von Mayer in 1842, tells us that energy in an isolated system, such as earth's biosphere, can be neither created nor destroyed. It can only be changed from one form to another. We see this principle playing out each day of our lives, perhaps without recognizing that we are surrounded by reminders of our enduring nature.

Thermal energy (heat), for example, which begins as sunlight, is used by plants to power the chemical energy (cells) that give them life. When the plants die, they can preserve the chemical energy they've embodied as the fossilized remains of the plant in the form of oil or coal. When the fossil fuels are burned, they convert the chemical energy back into heat energy to drive the turbines that produce electricity for our homes, factories, schools, and office buildings, or move the cylinders of an automobile engine. That heat energy, in turn, becomes the kinetic (moving) energy that gets us to work, school, or the store to buy groceries for our families.

The key point here is simply this: Throughout the entire cycle I've described, the energy was never created, and it was never destroyed. In each phase of the cycle, it simply changed form. This principle appears to be true for us as well.

As beings of energy, we always exist. Although we may change form and alter our expression, we cannot become "nothing." The best physics of the modern world tells us why it's literally impossible for us to disappear into nothingness. This foundational understanding weaves together the wisdom codes in this section: By reminding us of our eternal essence, we are led to a real-time understanding and a primal memory that it's literally impossible for our deepest fear of annihilation to materialize.

# Notes

---

---

---

---

---

---

---

---

---

---

---

---

---

---

# wisdom code 5

## Katha Upanishad

WISDOM CODE 5: The soul is not born, nor does it die. It did not spring from something, and nothing sprang from it. It is unborn, eternal, immortal, and ageless. It is not destroyed when the body is destroyed.

USE: This code addresses the uncertainty and universal fear that we cease to exist after death.

SOURCE: The Kathopanishad, sometimes known as the Katha Upanishad, one of the primary texts of the ancient Hindu Vedas, chapter 1, section 2, verses 18–2050

The collection of texts known as the Vedas is among the oldest scriptures of any of the world's major religions, dating to at least 3,000 years before the present, and possibly before. The texts were originally written in *Vedic Sanskrit,* the most ancient form of the ancient Sanskrit alphabet that is rarely used today. Vedic literature is a complex body of knowledge, and explanations of that knowledge have filled entire volumes and occupied the lives of scholars for centuries. For the purposes of this book, I've created the following brief description of how the Vedas are written and arranged to give a perspective for the source of this wisdom code.

The Vedas are traditionally viewed as a collection of four primary writings:

- The Rig Veda is comprised of 1,028 hymns and is the oldest Veda. It's dedicated to 33 deities worshipped at the time the texts were written.

- The Atharvaveda is comprised of 760 hymns describing the different modalities of healing that physicians of the day used.

- The Samaveda is a collection of 1,549 hymns that are believed to have been largely taken from the more inclusive Rig Veda, described previously. The text begins with hymns that are written to Agni, the god of fire, and Indra, the god of the heavens.

- The Yajurveda is comprised of over 1,800 mantras that describe religious rituals.

Each of these four bodies of writing contains portions known as the *Upanishads*—meaning they are *secret texts*—a classification that is based upon their content depicting mantras and ceremonies.

The source for Wisdom Code 5 is one of these Upanishads, the Kathopanishad, or Katha Upanishad, which is dedicated specifically to secrets of spirituality and meditation. With this classification in mind, the content of this wisdom code should come as no surprise. Regarding the universal fear of becoming nothing, it states:

*The soul is not born, nor does it die. It did not spring from something, and nothing sprang from it. It is unborn, eternal, immortal, and ageless. It is not destroyed when the body is destroyed.*

This wisdom code is among the most direct reminders of the unending nature of our essence. It also parallels Wisdom Code 7 from the Bhagavad Gita, which is a sacred Hindu text.

## HOW TO USE WISDOM CODE 5

The power of wisdom codes comes from their repetition and doing so in the affirmative. This imprints a code on the subconscious mind. When we create heart/brain harmony, as described in "How to Use the Wisdom Codes" (see page xix), we open a "hotline" to communicate directly with the subconscious mind.

From a place of heart/brain harmony, recite this code line by line, either silently in your mind or out loud, until you feel a shift in your sense of fear. The key is to embrace this code with a focus of awareness, breath, and feeling in the heart rather than the mind.

- *The soul is not born, nor does it die.*
- *It did not spring from something, and nothing sprang from it.*
- *It is unborn, eternal, immortal, and ageless.*
- *It is not destroyed when the body is destroyed.*

# Notes

_____

_____

_____

_____

_____

_____

_____

_____

_____

_____

_____

_____

# wisdom code 6

## Pyramid Texts

WISDOM CODE 6: There is no seed of a god which has perished, neither has he who belongs to him. You will not perish, who belongs to him.

USE: This code addresses the universal human fear of annihilation and the primal fear of nonexistence.

SOURCE: The Unas Pyramid Texts, utterance 213, verse 145

The hieroglyphs known as the Pyramid Texts from King Unas's pyramid in Egypt represent some of the oldest writings known to exist. I had the opportunity to explore the mysterious chambers of this pyramid and see them for myself in the fall of 1986 in the company of a small group of scientists and researchers. We made our way through the arch-topped passages and tunnels until we found ourselves in a single room with a vaulted ceiling that contains the now-famous hieroglyphic texts. These are chiseled, not painted, on the walls.

I found myself in awe of the texts for two reasons. One is that the instructions remain so well preserved today that they look as though the artist who created them could have finished and walked away only hours before. But beyond the extraordinary condition of the inscriptions, it's what they say that intrigued me the most.

## UTTERANCE 213

Of all the information that could have been written by the artist/scribe/priest who inscribed the chamber wall four millennia ago—from the climate change and extreme drought known to have existed at the time to the famine and social unrest that ancient records tell us plagued the era—the text mentions none of these things. Using a system of *utterances*, with each utterance consisting of multiple verses, the text is written with a single purpose in mind. It's designed to instruct, reassure, and comfort the soul of King Unas during its journey to the afterlife. Wisdom Code 6, taken from utterance 213, verse 145 of the Pyramid Texts, is a beautiful example that illustrates the nature of the reassurance that the ancient writings provide:

*There is no seed of a god which has perished, neither has he who belongs to him. You will not perish, who belongs to him.*

Through this ancient passage, the king's soul is reassured that—having originally emerged *from* a god and as a living expression *of* a god—its transition into the afterlife will be successful. *The soul cannot fail along its transition.* It is impossible to do so. Using the logic of the divine origin and the eternal nature of the soul, the text gives the king, or any religious initiate or scribe reading the texts, the reason to accept the assured success of his journey.

This ancient text is one of the earliest written examples of a technique that has been recognized throughout the centuries to instruct, aid, guide, comfort, and heal in times of need. And while the example from the Pyramid Texts was drafted in preparation for the death of King Unas 4,000 years ago, the principle is just as powerful, and works just as well, while we're still alive and facing the challenges of everyday life in our contemporary world. The power of the Pyramid Texts is "hidden" in the plain sight of a wisdom code that we have access to each day of our lives.

## HOW TO USE WISDOM CODE 6

The power of wisdom codes comes from their repetition and doing so in the affirmative. This imprints a code on the subconscious mind. When we create heart/brain harmony, as described in "How to Use the Wisdom Codes" (see page xix), we open a "hotline" to communicate directly with the subconscious mind.

From a place of heart/brain harmony, recite this code line by line, either silently in your mind or out loud, until you feel a shift in your sense of fear. The key is to embrace this code with a focus of awareness, breath, and feeling in the heart rather than the mind.

- *There is no seed of a god which has perished, neither has he who belongs to him.*

- *You will not perish, who belongs to him.*

# Notes

_____

_____

_____

_____

_____

_____

_____

_____

_____

_____

_____

_____

_____

_____

# Notes

_____

_____

_____

_____

_____

_____

_____

_____

_____

_____

_____

_____

_____

# wisdom code 7

## Bhagavad Gita

WISDOM CODE 7: The soul is never created, nor does it ever die. The soul is without birth, eternal, immortal, and ageless. It is not destroyed when the body is destroyed.

USE: This code addresses the universal human fear of annihilation and the primal fear of nonexistence.

SOURCE: Bhagavad Gita, chapter 2, verse 20

On the eve of the epic battle described in the Sanskrit scripture known as the Bhagavad Gita, the warrior and master archer Arjuna finds himself struggling with another kind of battle that he has not expected. It's not a physical battle of armor, spears, and arrows. Rather, it's a personal battle of conflicting emotions that have resulted from recognizing the dire consequences of leading his army into battle. As he looks out over the vast plain of Kurukshetra, the field where the legendary clash of two great armies is about to occur (located in the present-day Indian state of Haryana), he knows the battle will be epic in scale, as well as in the loss of human life.

The root of the conflict is the struggle between two cousins for access to the royal throne. On the eve of the battle, it's apparent that all diplomacy has failed. The source of inner conflict for Arjuna is that he realizes, as he gazes over the field, that the rival armies instructed to settle the dispute are composed of neighbors, friends, and family whom he has known his entire life.

## ARJUNA'S CHOICE

Recognizing that to engage in the battle will lead to an inevitable outcome of immense suffering, to the death of lifelong friends and relatives, Arjuna concludes that the material wealth of the throne is not worth the price of human lives. He makes the difficult choice as a warrior leader to back out of the battle. Arjuna places his powerful bow on the ground (a bow that is said on occasion to have released 30,000 arrows all at once) and refuses to lead his army toward such a tragic outcome. And this is where the philosophies that have made the Bhagavad Gita a cherished part of the Hindu sacred literature begin.

Arjuna shares his dilemma with his chariot driver and asks him for advice. What he does not know at the time is that his driver, Krishna, is really the Hindu god Vishnu who has temporarily taken on a human form so he can speak with Arjuna. Krishna sees that Arjuna is struggling because of his thinking regarding battle, life, death, and even reality itself.

Krishna begins a discourse with Arjuna that reveals a series of timeless truths that offer Arjuna comfort, reason, and hope in the face of life's greatest challenges. These philosophies are identified as the reasons that Krishna uses to persuade Arjuna to accept his fate as a warrior, and in doing so, to reverse his decision and lead his army into the battle.

I'm sharing this tale to provide context for Wisdom Code 7, lines that represent the first of Krishna's philosophical arguments. It's in this part of his conversation that Krishna reminds Arjuna that due to the immortal nature of the soul, everyone in the pending battle is eternal. This means that, ultimately, none of the warriors fighting on either side of the battle can be destroyed.

*The soul is never created, nor does it ever die.*

*The soul is without birth, eternal, immortal, and ageless.*

*It is not destroyed when the body is destroyed.*

Following this declaration of our eternal nature, Krishna then refines his argument through a series of increasingly detailed revelations regarding how the soul is eternal, and why, by deduction, we must be eternal as well. Through this explanation, he reassures Arjuna's heart, as well as his mind, that regardless of the outcome of the looming battle, everyone involved on either side will survive in some form.

Following are significant excerpts from Krishna's argument. These are not consecutively written in the original Sanskrit text.

*That which pervades the entire body you should know to be indestructible. No one is able to destroy that imperishable soul.*

*For the soul there is neither birth nor death at any time. He has not come into being, does not come into being, and will not come into being. He is unborn, eternal, ever existing, and primeval. He is not slain when his body is slain.*

*The soul can never be cut to pieces by any weapon, nor burned by fire, nor moistened by water, nor withered by the wind.*

*This individual soul is unbreakable and insoluble and can be neither burned nor dried. He is everlasting, present everywhere, unchangeable, immovable, and eternally the same.*

Arjuna listens carefully to Krishna's revelations. And in doing so, he discovers the true nature of the soul, the illusion of this world, and the existence of a greater, ultimate reality. Taking these newfound understandings into consideration, Arjuna changes his perspective regarding the battle at hand and his role in it. He accepts his role as a warrior within the broader context of good and evil. And from his new thinking, he proceeds to lead his army, made of the Pandava people, to victory against their cousins, the Kauravas, on the great plain of Kurukshetra. The rest, as they say, is history.

While historians cannot verify all the details described in the Bhagavad Gita, archaeological evidence does, in fact, suggest that the battle of Kurukshetra was real. The discovery of artifacts matching the descriptions in the texts suggests that fighting occurred at the location the Bhagavad Gita describes—a location that is still a revered sacred site in India today.

## HOW TO USE WISDOM CODE 7

The power of wisdom codes comes from their repetition and doing so in the affirmative. This imprints a code on the subconscious mind. When we create heart/brain harmony, as described in "How to Use the Wisdom Codes" (see page xix), we open a "hotline" to communicate directly with the subconscious mind.

From a place of heart/brain harmony, recite this code line by line, either silently in your mind or out loud, until you feel a shift in your sense of fear. The key is to embrace this code with a focus of awareness, breath, and feeling in the heart rather than the mind.

- *The soul is never created, nor does it ever die.*
- *The soul is without birth, eternal, immortal, and ageless.*
- *It is not destroyed when the body is destroyed.*

Notes

# wisdom code 8

## The Gospel of Peace

WISDOM CODE 8: One day your body will return to the Earthly Mother; even also your ears and your eyes. But the Holy Stream of Life, the Holy Stream of Sound, and the Holy Stream of Light, these were never born, and can never die.

USE: This code addresses the primal fear of non-existence and our relationship to a greater presence.

SOURCE TEXT: The Essene Gospel of Peace

Five hundred years before the birth of Jesus, a mysterious group of healer-scholars formed communities near the present-day Dead Sea in an area known as Qumran. The community included many religious sects, including the Nazarenes and the Ebionites, people known collectively as the *Essenes*. While the origin and nature of the Essenes remains controversial today, their existence is undisputed. Some of the first references to the lineage of the Essenes are found on clay tablets of ancient Sumer dating as far back as 3500 B.C.E. They're also recorded in historic writings that range from those of 1st-century Roman scholars Flavius Josephus and Pliny the Elder, where Essenes are referred to as a "race by themselves, more remarkable than any other in the world" in manuscripts preserved today in libraries and museums that include the Austrian National Library in Vienna, the British Museum in London, and the Vatican Library in Vatican City.

Elements of nearly every major religion of the world today, including those indigenous to China, Tibet, Egypt, India, Palestine, Greece, and the American desert Southwest, may be traced back to the original wisdom preserved by the Essenes. Many mystical traditions from the Western world, in particular, have roots in this body of information, such as the traditions of the Freemasons, Gnostic Christians, and Kabbalists. Wisdom Code 8 is derived from a collection of Essene texts that found their way safely from Palestine before the advance of the Mongol forces between 1299 and 1300 C.E., then into the hands of Nestorian priests in Asia, and ultimately into the Vatican Library. It was there, in the early 1920s, that student and scholar Edmond Bordeaux Szekely was given special access to the library for a research project. In the course of exploring the library for his thesis, he discovered the forgotten Aramaic gospel of Jesus's teachings. Although he was not allowed to remove the documents from the Vatican, he transcribed and later published excerpts of these documents as the book series the *Essene Gospel of Peace.*

## THE SACRED MARRIAGE

The principles of nature and natural laws are central to the teachings of the Essenes. In the language of the day, this mysterious sect, which is also believed to be the author of the Dead Sea Scrolls, offered a worldview that describes a holistic and unified relationship between the earth and our physical bodies. Through eloquent words that are our poetic reminders, the Essenes remind us that we are the product of a sacred union—*a marriage*—between the mysterious, unformed, eternal essence of the soul and the physical matter of this world.

From the perspective of this marriage, we are part of, and intimately enmeshed with, all that we see as our world. Every rock, every tree, and each mountain, every river and ocean is a part of us, and we a part of it. Perhaps most importantly, because of this union, we're each a part of one another.

The Essene Gospel of Peace is a record of Jesus describing the relationship between our "Mother Earth" and our "Father in Heaven." According to the text, the union that gives us life originated as follows: "The spirit of the Son of Man was created from the spirit of the Heavenly Father, and his body from the body of the Earthly Mother."

This Essene description of life parallels the perspective that we have seen in the previous wisdom codes: there is a part of us that has always existed, cannot be formed or destroyed, and exists eternally as the Essene Holy Stream of Life.

Wisdom Code 8 reads:

> *One day your body will return to the Earthly Mother;*
> *even also your ears and your eyes. But the Holy Stream of*
> *Life, the Holy Stream of Sound, and the Holy Stream of*
> *Light, these were never born, and can never die.*

In another section of the Essene Gospel of Peace, our relationship to the Holy Stream is clarified in unmistakable terms: "And you shall be one with the Holy Stream of Light, always before you sleep in the arms of the Heavenly Father."

The power of Wisdom Code 8 is twofold. First it reminds us of the timeless and eternal nature of our essence. In this reminder, the text appeals to both our heart and our intellect, as we are given the reason to dispel our anxiety and fears of becoming nothing, and forever lost in existence.

The second reason this wisdom code is so effective is because of the parallel between the Essene perspective and those of the Bhagavad Gita, sacred hieroglyphs from Egyptian death cults, the Vedic Upanishads, and other world spiritual traditions. Each of us learns differently. Due to our personal cultural, familial, and religious background, we may find ourselves more comfortable with a Buddhist perspective than we are with a Hindu text, or more comfortable with Christian literature than the markings carved into the rock wall of an Egyptian tomb. Herein we find the beauty of Wisdom Code 8. In a direct and conversational way, using the analogy of a human mother and father, we are reminded of the powerful message of our eternal nature.

## HOW TO USE WISDOM CODE 8

The power of wisdom codes comes from their repetition and doing so in the affirmative. This imprints a code on the subconscious mind. When we create heart/brain harmony, as described in "How to Use the Wisdom Codes" (see page xix), we open a "hotline" to communicate directly with the subconscious mind.

From a place of heart/brain harmony, recite this code line by line, either silently in your mind or out loud, until you feel a shift in your sense of fear. The key is to embrace this code with a focus of awareness, breath, and feeling in the heart rather than the mind.

- *One day your body will return to the Earthly Mother; even also your ears and your eyes.*

- *But the Holy Stream of Life, the Holy Stream of Sound, and the Holy Stream of Light, these were never born, and can never die.*

# Notes

# PART THREE

# loss

*The greatest loss is what dies inside us while we live.*

— Norman Cousins, political journalist

Loss is a universal experience.

It's inevitable. It's inescapable. And it's natural. We all lose something each day of our lives. Sometimes our losses are so subtle that they're almost imperceptible. From the time we're young, for example, we see "progress" changing the faces of the homes, streets, grocery stores, and movie theaters that we grew up with. While the incremental change of a new mall or the loss of our favorite late-night café may seem insignificant as it occurs, when we put those changes together and look backward in time, we find that the way we remember our neighborhood is barely recognizable when compared to the current version of our surroundings.

And although our logic tells us that it's natural for our surroundings to change, we rarely give our emotions the opportunity to catch up and adjust to the shift. In our culture, we're expected to just "go with the flow" and embrace the transformation. The truth is, however, that we need time to adjust. We need time to acclimate to the void that the loss of familiar things leaves in our lives and in our hearts.

While the loss of familiar surroundings rarely brings our everyday activities to a screeching halt, there are other kinds of loss that do—such as the loss of a child, a life partner, a parent, or a beloved friend or colleague. Even when we know in advance that our loved one is imminently leaving this world and we've prepared ourselves for the loss, all the preparation in the world does not stop the pain. Loss hurts. The pain is very real, and the reason for the pain is what makes this group of wisdom codes so powerful.

## WHY LOSS HURTS

When a loved one is with us in body, there is an energy that we create from the merging of our awareness, consciousness, and feelings for one another. More than a metaphor, this very real and measurable field of energy results from the bioelectric, biomagnetic, and photonic fields that we emit from the cells of our blood, organs, and tissues. We know this energy as the feeling we experience when we meet a lover or dear friend, for example, at a café for tea or coffee. The instant we see them, our eyes light up, we have a big smile on our face, and we tingle as our energy comes alive.

And just as a really great batch of cacao peanut butter cookies reflects the quality, as well as the quantity, of the ingredients that we place into the mix, it's that sparkle, smile, glow, and tingle that reveals the one-of-a-kind energy that we create in the presence of our loved ones. And it's precisely *because* this field of energy is so very real that when it dissolves with their passing we experience so much hurt. When we lose a loved one, the field of energy that we've created together begins to disintegrate. It has to, because the energy from the body that once held it together no longer exists.

Just as water and sugar merge into a fluid system when they are combined, in our emotion-based relationships, the fields that we create are fluid and malleable. A field changes with our moods, pace and quality of communication, and depth of trust. And just as the system of sugar and water begins to change if the water evaporates, our relationship energy begins to take on a new form in the absence of a loved one—particularly someone who has died. We often hear people reflect this fact, saying things like it's as though something has been "ripped away" from them, or that they feel incomplete and "empty" when they lose someone close. They're telling us the truth. The emptiness is real. And it results from the loss of the energy that was once created in the absent person's presence—even sometimes at a distance.

## EMBRACING FINALITY

It's the feeling of finality that defines the power of loss in our lives. When we lose a loved one, we sense that finality as we realize that the body we once touched, held, laughed and cried over no longer exists. Our senses struggle with the fact that in one moment someone is with us in the world, breathing the same air that we breathe and sharing all the things that define our human condition, and then, in the next moment, they're gone. It's the emotional finality of our loss that confronts us head on, and promises that we will never be the same.

Our feelings are telling us the truth. It's literally impossible for us to ever be the same, because our loved one was the catalyst for a way of being that can no longer exist. It's the hugeness of this realization and the degree to which we embrace the depth of its meaning that determine the power we will find in our grief. Once we accept these facts and embrace their meaning, we find ourselves at the crossroad of choosing one of two powerful paths.

On one path, we deny our grief. In our denial, we attempt to live each day as if we are the same person, living in the same world as we did before we lost our loved one. On the second path, we accept our grief. And in our acceptance, we open the door to the healing that grief brings to our doorstep. It's in our willingness to accept our loss that we heal.

## LOSS AS A TEACHER OF LOVE

The Greek philosopher Aristotle noted: "Nature abhors a vacuum." His statement was based upon his observation that nature does not allow anything to be empty for long. Grass grows when trees are removed from a hillside; air fills a vessel when the water it once contained is removed; and the perfect balance that we strive to maintain in our lives will be upset by nature's prime directive to create movement and change. Modern science supports Aristotle's observation. The equations that describe fractal systems, for example, confirm that balance will give way to chaos in search of a higher order of balance. It is the same with the vacuum in our lives created by the loss of someone who we love and care for. New relationships blossom and grow to fill the void of lost parents, friends, and lovers.

There's an unspoken potential that each of us will lose the people and the ways of life that we cherish and hold most dear. It's inevitable because nothing lasts forever. It's this fact that promises we will experience loss in our lives, and the grief that is the consequence, as well as the path to healing from loss. Whether it's the loss of a friend or loved one, or the loss of a community and an entire way of life, the result is the same. Grief is nature's support system for reconciling loss and helping us to move forward with life in a healthy way. It's also nature's way to get us to feel our grief even when we may be reluctant to do so.

The only way to heal from loss is to feel what the absence of something or someone we love means in our lives. There's a direct relationship between the emotional trauma of grief and the degree that we allow ourselves to feel our loss. The relationship is this: The deeper the hurt, the more powerful the feelings, and the deeper we must reach inside of ourselves to find the love that will enable us to transcend the hurt. It's through our grief that we discover a deeper, and sometimes surprising, capacity to love.

Ancient people identified ways of thinking about loss that made it easier to feel and grieve. These perspectives couldn't change the source of life's deepest hurts. They couldn't change the fact that husbands were lost in battle, wives were lost giving birth, and mysterious diseases took friends and loved ones in the prime of life. Rather, as they invited the wisdom codes of their traditions into their lives, they discovered a healthy perspective that allowed them to transcend the losses they endured.

## A SOLO JOURNEY

Through the grief that follows loss, we temporarily experience emotional and physiological shock. And even when we're surrounded by the best-intentioned friends and loved ones, and receiving support, just as it is with fear, as described in Part Two, we ultimately go through the gauntlet of grief alone. No one can grieve for us. Grief is a solo journey.

And that journey often leads us to a battleground within ourselves where we discover conflicting emotions and the feeling of being empty, numb, and isolated.

With our conflicted emotions come the seemingly endless questions that loop tirelessly in our mind: among them, *Will I ever feel better? What do I do now? Why is this happening?*

There is a strength that can only be known in the presence of loss and grief. And with that strength comes the reward of life's deepest levels of personal mastery.

# Notes

_____

_____

_____

_____

_____

_____

_____

_____

_____

_____

_____

_____

_____

# wisdom code 9

## Otagaki Rengetsu

WISDOM CODE 9: The impermanence of this floating world I feel over and over. It is hardest to be the one left behind.

USE: This code reminds us that even in the knowledge that all things are temporary, enduring the loss of a loved one is still one of hardest things we will face.

SOURCE TEXT: Otagaki Rengetsu, renowned Buddhist nun

The principle of impermanence recognizes that we live in a dynamic world of constant change, and it is precisely because nothing is static that we can expect nothing to last forever.

## LOSS FROM THE BUDDHIST PERSPECTIVE

To ease our suffering in times of loss, Buddhist teachings invite us to consider our pain within the larger context of a universal template for human experience. The template is known as the *three marks of existence*, which are identified as follows:

- Impermanence
- Suffering
- The non-self

Briefly stated, when we are suffering, the cause of our pain is attachment: our expectation that something, some place, or someone will continue to exist in a way that meets our expectations. The third mark of existence, embracing the non-self, is the solution to transcend our suffering. The non-self is defined as a state of enlightenment that is achieved through the release of our personal identity—the ego self—in exchange for a greater all-inclusive identity. In this expanded identity, we view ourselves as part of, rather than separate from, the world around us. By embracing this more mindful version of ourselves, we are freed from the suffering that is the result of attachment.

## A BUDDHIST NUN'S PERSPECTIVE

The teachings of Buddhism typically refer us to the words and remedies of the Buddha himself when it comes to healing the suffering from the loss of a loved one. Wisdom Code 9 offers us something different. While its roots are firmly planted in Buddhist philosophy, the code invites us *beyond* the obvious reminders that we live in a world of impermanence and suffering. While acknowledging these truths, the code goes deeper and invites us to embrace a more intimate and exclusively human dimension of what we endure in our loss.

This wisdom code is attributed to Otagaki Rengetsu, a Buddhist nun born in 1791. In addition to becoming a nun later in her life, Rengetsu was also a renowned potter, expert calligrapher, and respected painter, as well as one of the 19th century's great poets. Wisdom Code 9 is an example of her work, and in it she encapsulates two of the foundational Buddhist principles.

*The impermanence of this floating world I feel over and over.*

*It is hardest to be the one left behind.*

A close examination of this code reveals the elegance of its meaning, and the power that it conveys in its conciseness. Excerpted from the book *Rengetsu: Life and Poetry of Lotus Moon* compiled by translator John Stevens, the first line of the poem follows the template of traditional Buddhist thinking and reminds us of the temporary nature of all things:

*The impermanence of this floating world I feel over and over.*

After stating the fact of life's impermanence, however, in the next line she reveals why she's feeling the repeated impact of loss. The reason is that all things, regardless of how old, how reliable, how sustainable, or how loved, are temporary at best. It's precisely because of the temporary nature of all things, including our loved ones, that Rengetsu says she experiences impermanence "over and over." As do we all. Each time we bear the suffering that results from the void created by our loss, we are reminded of a universal certainty: We live in a world where nothing lasts forever.

The second line of the poem is where Rengetsu deviates from the traditional Buddhist objectivity of an observer to the humanness of an experiencer. She expresses a universal feeling when she states what the impermanence she experiences means to her on a very intimate level:

*It is hardest to be the one left behind.*

Here we get the sense that she is speaking from the truth of personal experience, and in doing so, speaking for us collectively. Even knowing that nothing lasts forever, the most difficult part of the journey of loss is when we find ourselves left behind, as our loved ones disappear as a result of their impermanence.

The power of this wisdom code is that in voicing the deep truth of our loss, we are acknowledging our inner pain. And it's precisely this acknowledgment that frees us from being stuck in our emotions, while awakening our healing.

## HOW TO USE WISDOM CODE 9

The power of wisdom codes comes from their repetition and doing so in the affirmative. This imprints a code on the subconscious mind. When we create heart/brain harmony, as described in "How to Use the Wisdom Codes" (see page xix), we open a "hotline" to communicate directly with the sub-conscious mind.

From a place of heart/brain harmony, recite this code line by line, either silently in your mind or out loud, until you feel a shift in your sense of grief. The key is to embrace this code with a focus of awareness, breath, and feeling in the heart rather than the mind.

- *The impermanence of this floating world I feel over and over.*

- *It is hardest to be the one left behind.*

# Notes

_____

_____

_____

_____

_____

_____

_____

_____

_____

_____

_____

_____

_____

# wisdom code 10

## Buddha

WISDOM CODE 10: You only lose what you cling to.

USE: This code reminds us that our suffering in times of loss is the result of our attachment to what is impermanent.

SOURCE: A widely used, colloquial summary of the Buddhist principle of nonattachment

From the DNA in our cells and the relationships in our lives to the societies we live in, we're part of a living universe that's in constant motion, appearing, disappearing, and creating dynamic change. Buddhism reminds us that our experience of loss comes from our perceptions of life, surroundings, and relationships within the context of that change. As we discovered in Part Two, "Fear," it's impossible for anything to truly disappear in the sense that it no longer exists—as in annihilation. When we feel that we've lost someone or something, it's less about their disappearance in the world and more about our perception of their disappearance.

Our relationships in life are a dance of energy. They are timeless and constant. Sometimes consciously, and often not, the partners who dance with us will lead us to achieve our greatest possible destiny, or to succumb to the depths of our fate. The key here is that the agreement is based upon synergies that overlap in a moment of time. The expectation that our synergy will continue, unchanged, throughout time—our attachment to lasting nature of the harmony—is why we suffer when it does not.

## BALANCE VS. HARMONY

It never fails. Just when you think you've created a perfect balance in your life—when you've checked the virtual boxes on your mental list for the perfect relationship, the perfect job, the perfect home, and the perfect economic plan for your future—something pops up seemingly from nowhere and changes everything. And while you may be surprised, Mother Nature isn't.

As we discovered previously, what we experience as balance is a temporary state of *harmony* that occurs in a world of constant flux. There's a powerful distinction between balance and harmony. In a system of perfect balance, nothing can happen. Nothing can move and nothing can change because in perfect balance, there is no change. For this reason, balance rarely happens; and when it does, it's fleeting. Nature is dynamic. In nature, the achievement of balance in a system is the trigger that initiates change in that system.

For example, it's not a balance of wildlife that maintains an ecosystem. In a forest there is rarely a perfect balance between predators and prey. There cannot be—the size, location, and resilience of various populations is always changing. Rather, nature strives for *harmony* in the system. It's the shifting *harmony* between coyotes and rabbits, for example, or birds and insects, that keeps the populations in check, even though their relative size is always changing. The imbalance in the system is what becomes the trigger for change.

In a similar way, the balance that you may think you're striving for in life is probably more about harmony: harmony between family and career, harmony between leisure and work, and harmony between partnerships and friends. And the key to harmony is to make room for change in your life. It's this principle that is the underlying theme of Wisdom Code 10. This code reflects a traditional Buddhist thinking.

## WISDOM CODE 10: THE SOURCE

Although Wisdom Code 10 is often represented as a direct quote from the Buddha, this is not true. While the wording of this code supports Buddha's teachings, to the best of this author's knowledge, there is no book, chapter, or verse from an ancient Sanskrit text that states these words. Rather, Wisdom Code 10 is a commonly used summary of the Buddhist principle of nonattachment and what it means in times of loss. This code provides a new perspective regarding loss, and how to heal the suffering from our loss, via the *three marks of existence* described previously in Wisdom Code 9.

In summary, the *first mark of existence* directly states the impermanence of all things and reminds us that all things, all people, and all relationships are temporary. The *second mark of existence* directly states that our suffering is the result of our attachment to people, relationships, and conditions that are, by their very nature, temporary. The *third mark of existence* is implied as a conclusion of the first two marks. It's also the source for the power and healing that is possible from Wisdom Code 10.

The third mark of existence is known as the *doctrine of non-self* (*anatman* in Sanskrit). It states that the key to healing in our time of loss is to relinquish the aspect of ourselves that's experiencing the suffering—the ego self that wants our friendships, relationships, families, and life circumstances to remain in a static existence. We do so by embracing the greater expression of ourselves as the non-self. In this new and expanded identity, we view ourselves as part of, rather than separate from, the world around us. As part of all that we know and experience, it's impossible to really lose anything.

## HEALING TWO ILLUSIONS

By embracing the more mindful version of ourselves offered in the third mark of existence, we initiate our healing from two illusions—the illusions that (1) we ever really have another person, that we really "own" a place, a pet, or the land that we live on; and (2) our habit of clinging to someone or something as a permanent fixture in our lives—we change what the experience of loss means to us. In doing so, we ultimately give new meaning to the suffering that comes from our loss.

Just to be absolutely clear, this wisdom code is not an invitation to be indifferent to the losses that we will inevitably experience in our life. It's not intended to discount or in any way deny the hurt that we feel from the loss of a friend, pet, or loved one. It is intended to ease the burden of our losses when they occur.

The power of Wisdom Code 10 is that it gives us a reason to think differently about the people, places, and things that leave us. We can't change the leaving. When we find ourselves in loss, we face one of two choices. Either we can remain stuck in our feelings of the wrongness, failure, and the tragedy of what we've lost, or we can accept our loss and allow for the healing that's necessary to fill the void.

## HOW TO USE WISDOM CODE 10

Wisdom Code 10 is an informal statement reminding us of the source of our suffering in times of loss, as well as the remedy to transcend our suffering. The power of wisdom codes comes from their repetition and doing so in the affirmative. This imprints a code on the subconscious mind. When we create heart/brain harmony, as described in "How to Use the Wisdom Codes" (see page xix), we open a "hotline" to communicate directly with the subconscious mind.

From a place of heart/brain harmony, recite this code, either silently in your mind or out loud, until you feel a shift in the sense of grief from your loss. You may choose between the original template (you voice) or the personalized template (I voice). The key is to embrace this code with a focus of awareness, breath, and feeling in the heart rather than the mind.

## The Original Wisdom Code Template

- *You only lose what you cling to.*

## The Personalized Wisdom Code Template

- *I only lose what I cling to.*

# Notes

_____

_____

_____

_____

_____

_____

_____

_____

_____

_____

_____

_____

# Notes

_____

_____

_____

_____

_____

_____

_____

_____

_____

_____

_____

_____

_____

# wisdom code 11

## Pavamana Mantra

WISDOM CODE 11: Lead me from the unreal to the real. Lead me from the darkness to the light. Lead me from death to immortality. Let there be peace, peace, peace.

USE: This code is in the form of a chant or a mantra, designed to help us in times of loss and mourning.

SOURCE: Brihadaranyaka Upanishad

For nearly 3,000 years, the ancient Upanishads have remained as a primary source of comfort, healing, and wisdom in the Hindu tradition. The power of these texts and the healing that they offer us in our times of loss is found in the name of the texts themselves. In Sanskrit, the word *Upanishad* means "to be *near*" (*upa*) and "to *sit*" (*ni-sad),* which literally reflects the way the Vedic wisdom was originally offered—to those sitting in the presence of a master.

One of the reasons that these texts have been held in such high esteem for nearly three millennia is because rather than offering a doctrine of structured information from an unseen and otherworldly source, these texts reflect wisdom gleaned by learned teachers—fellow humans sharing real experiences and their personal lives.

Wisdom Code 11, the *Pavamana Mantra*, is found in the Brihadaranyaka, one of the principal Upanishads, and is a treatise dedicated to the concept of the *atman*—the Hindu concept of the soul or the self. According to Professor John Campbell, a former professor of religious studies at the University of Virginia, this mantra speaks to the "transformation of the individual and their environment." And transformation is precisely what healing personal loss is all about.

In the presence of the emotional vacuum created by the loss of something or someone we love, we are changed. We will no longer continue in the world as the same person we were the moment before the loss occurred. We cannot, because the formula that defined the world as we've known it, which included our loved one, has changed. In that change we find our struggle. In the resolution of our struggle we discover our new identity. This is where Wisdom Code 11 can be a powerful catalyst in our healing. A closer look at this chant and the meaning of each statement provides the keys that help us to recognize, and embrace, the power of this Vedic wisdom in times of loss.

### Line 1: Lead me from the unreal to the real.

This statement is an invitation to the reader (chanter) to allow the deepest truth of the illusory nature of life—the unreal—to give way to what we already know in our heart is the real, yet transitory, nature of the world, our surroundings, and the lives of our loved ones.

### Line 2: Lead me from the darkness to the light.

This statement is a reminder that just as illusion (something unreal) gives way to the true nature of the world (the real), the darkness and suffering that comes from our losses gives way to the acceptance and healing (light) of the true nature of our essence.

### Line 3: Lead me from death to immortality.

Through this statement we see the completion of a hierarchy that began with the first phrase, and in that hierarchy, a deeper and more intimate application of our healing. The sequence leads us from the macro vision of the cosmos and the nature of reality, to the everyday components of darkness and light that power the reality of this world, to an intimate and micro perspective of darkness and light in our lives, expressed as death and immortality.

**Line 4: Let there be peace, peace, peace.**

This statement is the completion and closure of the chant and the goal of its application. As there is no exact translation in English for Sanskrit, while the original word that closes this chant, *shaantih*, can mean "peace," it also can mean "calm," "rest," or "tranquility." Each of these reflects the goal of coming to terms with the losses we experience in life.

## HOW TO USE WISDOM CODE 11

The power of wisdom codes comes from their repetition and doing so in the affirmative. This imprints a code on the subconscious mind. When we create heart/brain harmony, as described in "How to Use the Wisdom Codes" (see page xix), we open a "hotline" to communicate directly with the subconscious mind.

From a place of heart/brain harmony, recite this code line by line, either silently in your mind or chanting out loud, until you feel a shift in your sense of grief. The key is to embrace this code with a focus of awareness, breath, and feeling in the heart rather than the mind.

Some people find that reciting mantras from the Upanishads in the original Sanskrit offers an even greater healing when they use this ancient mantra. Following is the code in its entirety, first stated in English, followed by the words in Sanskrit.

### English Translation

- *Lead me from the unreal to the real.*
- *Lead from the darkness to the light.*

- *Lead me from death to immortality.*
- *Let there be peace, peace, peace.*

## Original Sanskrit Words

- *Om Asato Maa Sad-Gamaya.*
- *Tamaso Maa Jyotir-Gamaya.*
- *Mrtyor-Maa Amrtam Gamaya.*
- *Om Shaantih Shaantih Shaantih.*

# Notes

_____

_____

_____

_____

_____

_____

_____

_____

_____

_____

_____

_____

_____

# PART FOUR

# strength

*Go within every day and find the inner strength
so that the world will not blow your candle out.*

— KATHERINE DUNHAM,
ANTHROPOLOGIST AND DANCER

"You have now found the conditions in which the desire of your heart can become the reality of your being. Stay here until you acquire *a force* in you that nothing can destroy." With these words, a mysterious monk revealed the great source of power that awaits each of us as we embrace our inner potential for emotional strength.

The student receiving the message was 19th-century explorer and mystic George Ivanovich Gurdjieff, often known simply as Gurdjieff. His teacher was a member of the mysterious Sarmoung Brotherhood, a legendary and mystical sect that Gurdjieff sought out and located hidden deep in the mountains of Central Asia. The condition that the teacher was describing is the power of *inner strength* that is available to each of us, and the *choice* that Gurdjieff made to tap that force to achieve his greatest potential.

## CHOICE AND INNER STRENGTH

There is a direct relationship between our inner strength and the act of choice. That relationship reminds us that regardless of our life challenges, we always have the power to choose how we respond to what life brings to our doorstep. And it's the power of our choices that are the source of our inner strength. Without this power, it's easy to feel stuck, helpless, and trapped in our circumstances.

Before Gurdjieff could embark upon his long-sought-after mystical path to reveal his deepest strengths, a shift in his thinking had to happen. He had to (1) choose to allow his current belief system to be replaced by the knowledge that the Sarmoung Brotherhood revealed and (2) choose to allow that knowledge to become the wisdom that directed his life. In doing so, Gurdjieff exercised what are perhaps the two greatest, though perhaps also the least understood, powers of the human experience—the powers of choice and free will. These powers are intimately related and go hand in hand to become the source of our inner strength.

## FREE WILL: ILLUSION OR REAL?

Modern science suggests that free will is a uniquely human experience. To the best of our knowledge, no other form of life on earth has the ability to ponder the options available to them in a given moment—to ask "What if?" when it comes to considering the implications of their options—and then to choose an option based upon what they've considered. Clearly, our power of choice is a significant characteristic of our humanness. It's also the key to our highest levels of mastery.

For the purpose of this section, I'll define *free will* as our capacity to select from the myriad possibilities that exist in a given situation, and to then implement what we've chosen. In this context, we exercise our power of free will through the choices we make in each moment of every day of our lives— the food we choose to nourish our bodies; the way we choose to think of, and treat, other people; the way we choose to allow other people to treat us; our choice to give love without conditions, and our choice to receive the love that comes to us. The topic of choice, and how much choice we really have in life, has been, and remains today, the source of heated debate in academic and philosophical circles.

According to one scientific perspective, we really don't have any free will at all. Proponents of this school of thought base their opinion on the evidence for the big bang being the origin of the universe. Because all matter was initially connected in a moment of singularity, and the expansion that began with this singularity continues today, then the actions and interaction of all matter in the universe are determined by the events set into motion in a fraction of a second after the big bang, they say. We only *appear* to have free will because there are so many possibilities available to us in any given moment that we'll probably never run out of choices, and to us, the choices feel like they're infinite.

Another school of scientific thought suggests that rather than living in a deterministic and ordered universe that was set into motion at the instant of its creation, we live in a chaotic universe. From this perspective, there is no universal order and our choices are truly random and infinite within the context of the laws of physics that govern our physical world.

While both perspectives have scientific evidence to support them, to explore them in depth is more than I can do justice to in this brief introduction to Part Four. For this reason, my use of the term *free will* is meant to describe our decision to follow a course of action within the context of what we know is possible in each situation. Once we acknowledge the existence of choice and free will and the roles they play in our lives, the question becomes, how do we make use of such powers?

That is the issue that the next three wisdom codes help us address.

## Notes

# wisdom code 12

## Beauty Prayer

WISDOM CODE 12: The beauty that you live with, the beauty that you live by, the beauty upon which you base your life.

USE: This key reminds us that beauty exists in all things. Our job is to find the beauty in the experiences of life.

SOURCE: An informal version of an ancient Navajo prayer

Four hundred years ago in the high deserts of the American Southwest, the great wisdom keepers of the Navajo (*Diné*) families were tested by the extremes of climate, the elements, and the warring tribes that surrounded them. Through the hardships that resulted from drought, intense heat, and lack of food in their societies, the Navajo realized that they must transform the power of their *inner* pain to endure and transcend the harsh conditions of their *outer* world. Their very survival depended upon learning to do so.

Recognizing that life's tests pushed them to the greatest depths of their suffering, they also discovered that the same tests revealed their greatest strengths. The key to their survival was to immerse themselves fully in life's challenges, rather than attempting to avoid them, and to do so without becoming lost in the experience. They had to find the emotional anchors within themselves—the core beliefs that gave them the strength to endure their tests—and the knowledge that a better day would follow. From this place of inner power, they had the confidence to take risks and implement the changes to thrive in their changing world.

## FINDING AN EMOTIONAL ANCHOR

Our lives today may not be so very different from the lives of native people that roamed the high deserts of North America long ago. Although the scenery has shifted and the circumstances have changed, we still find ourselves in situations that shake the foundation of our beliefs, test the limits of our sensibilities, and challenge us to rise above the things that hurt us.

From cable television news cycles that bombard us with world tragedies on a 24/7 basis and the impact of a changing climate, to the dysfunction of social and political policies that seem to make no sense, it's easy to get swept into the emotional chaos of celebrities, friends, family, and co-workers caught in the drama of life's extremes. These are precisely the times when we need a way of thinking that leads to a more balanced and healthier perspective—an emotional compass to keep us on a steady path. The ancient wisdom codes that served the Navajo in their day can do the same for us today if we invite those codes into our lives.

## THE HIDDEN POWER OF BEAUTY

Recent discoveries in modern science now add to a growing body of evidence suggesting that beauty is more than simply a pleasurable aesthetic; it's a transformative power. More than simply an adjective that describes the colors of a sunset, or a rainbow following a late-summer storm, beauty is a direct, sensual, and life-altering experience—specifically, beauty is *our* experience. Humans are believed to be the only species of life on Earth with the capability of perceiving beauty in the world around them and seeking beauty within the experiences of our everyday lives.

Through our experience of beauty, we're given the power to change what we feel in our body. As described previously, our feelings, in turn, are directly linked to the way neurons "wire and fire," and to the chemistry of our cells and organs, as well as the world beyond our body. So when we say that beauty has the power to change our lives, it's no exaggeration to say that the same beauty also has the power to change our world! The key is that we must choose to look beyond the hurt, suffering, and pain that we're presented with in the moment and recognize the beauty that already exists in all things. Only then will we have unleashed the power that the choice of beauty holds for our lives.

## THE NAVAJO BEAUTY PRAYER

Through an eloquence that's typical of such ancient wisdom, Navajo tradition describes a way of looking at life's extremes that places the responsibility for our happiness, as well as our suffering, squarely upon our shoulders. Wisdom Code 12 reflects this perspective and is known as the Beauty Prayer. This powerful code forms the closing prayer of the Blessing Way ceremony, one of a series of six ceremonies intended to bring harmony to the cosmos and all things in it. Other ceremonies in the series include the Holy Ways, the Life Ways, the Evil Ways, the War Ceremonials, and the Game Ways. Although the precise language of Wisdom Code 12 varies from transcription to transcription, and from telling to telling as it is handed down from generation to generation, the theme of the prayer remains unchanged.

To offer the essence of this code as simply and respectfully as possible, I'm sharing an informal daily-use version that was described by the Navajo artist and painter Shonto Begay in a magazine article I read many years ago. Begay offers the code in three brief phrases, with each phrase illuminating a key insight into our power to shift the chemistry of the body and influence the way we see our world. I also offer a longer, more formal version of the prayer in the text that immediately follows this description.

Begay describes the essence of the Navajo beauty prayer, stating "We say nizhonigoo bil iina, the beauty that you live with, the beauty that you live by, the beauty upon which you base your life." Through these words, for centuries Navajo elders have conveyed a sophisticated wisdom, reminding their people, and now us, of the connection between our inner and outer worlds—a connection that has been recognized only recently by modern science. Each phrase of this prayer describes one facet of our relationship with beauty, and what the embrace of beauty can mean to our lives. The key here is that we must invite the power of beauty into our lives. A closer look at this wisdom code, phrase by phrase, reveals the subtle nuances of the prayer and why it holds so much power.

### Phrase 1: "The beauty that you live with"

This phrase is a key to remind us that we don't create the beauty that is present in the world. It already exists. And while not all things are necessarily beautiful, there is a beauty that may be found in all things and in every situation. Our job is to find that beauty—to seek it out even when it's not apparent. To do so is a choice. From the deeply personal loss of loved ones to the crises of health and relationship that appear in our lives, finding beauty is the key to making sense of the seemingly senseless events of life. In addition to the wisdom of the ancient Navajo, we're given living examples of the power of our choices by great masters today.

The Catholic saint Mother Teresa is a perfect example of what I mean here. Mother Teresa, or "Mother" as those close to this great woman called her, applied the simple elegance of her belief in beauty to her life. In doing so, she forever changed the ancient stigma attached to the so-called untouchables of India, the unclaimed, diseased, and dying people that are often found abandoned in the streets. Without judging them as "less than" anyone else, she and her Missionaries of Charity volunteers would go out each morning to search the streets of Calcutta for the people whom they called God's children. The sisters would take these people, historically shunned by Indian society, and sometimes even their own families, to the hospices that they created to give them dignity and privacy and beauty in their last remaining hours on earth. In doing so

Mother Teresa would find beauty where few people believed that beauty could exist.

Amid the filth of garbage and debris in the gutters, the stench and decay of rotting food and unidentifiable carcasses in the alleys, she would notice a mass of cow dung in the street. Growing in the dung, she would find a colorful flower. In that flower she would find life, and in that life she found beauty—she chose to see beauty—in the streets of Calcutta. This is the power of choice that we're given when it comes to how we see life.

Each time we choose to see the beauty that's possible or already present in the hurt, loss, disappointments, and betrayals of life, we are making the choice to take back our power rather than be defined by the situation. When we say, "The beauty that I live with" (the word *you* may be replaced with *I* to make the prayer more personal), we are acknowledging this fact and making the choice to see the beauty that exists in everything.

### Phrase 2: "The beauty that you live by"

The second line of the prayer reminds us of the significant role that beauty may play in our lives. When we live searching for and expecting to discover beauty in everything that life shows us, we begin to see the polarities of the world, and ourselves, in a new light. While we can't change what has already happened, as we acknowledge life's tragedies, we also recognize that within each experience there is a beauty that balances the extremes.

Mother Teresa was a master at inviting beauty into her life on a daily basis. Her life gives us a beautiful template to do the same.

### Phrase 3: "The beauty upon which you base your life"

This next phrase is a code that guides us beyond simply finding the beauty that exists in all things. It leads us to the next step of giving that beauty greater significance in our life. With no words of explanation, no rationalization, and no justification, great masters such as Mother Teresa *choose* to see beauty everywhere and in all things. To them, it was already present. It was everywhere, always. Through their lives, we're reminded that our job is to discover that beauty. Life is our opportunity to seek beauty and to embrace the beauty that we discover in all things—from the deepest hurts to the greatest joys—to become the standard to which we hold our lives and ourselves.

When we base our life upon the principle of beauty and allow it to become the foundation of our worldview, we are changed as people. Our choice to do so replaces our hurt, hopelessness, and fear with the transformative power that beauty makes possible. And it's not just our imagination. Our willingness to embrace the beauty in all things literally directs our neurons to reflect our choice. Our cells begin to seek other cells that hold the same chemical balance and connect to create the new neural pathways that elevate our perspective above the fray of the experience. Through the words of a Navajo author whose name was forgotten long ago, which have been handed down from person to person and through ceremony after ceremony for centuries, the power and simplicity of this prayer offers renewed hope when all else seems to fail.

## THE FULL TRANSLATION OF THE NAVAJO BEAUTY PRAYER

In the previous section, I identified a brief and simplified version of the beauty prayer, offered by Shonto Begay. In this section, I want to share a formal version of the same prayer. Both versions may function as Wisdom Code 12.

In times of need, when I find myself reeling from the shock of a world tragedy or the loss of a loved one, or I'm feeling the emotional impact of a difficult relationship, I typically use the brief form of the Beauty Prayer as my go-to version because I don't need to look it up or read it from a printed sheet. It's brief, direct, and powerful as it is.

In a more formal setting, however, such as when I'm leading a large audience in a prayer, or in the leisure of an extended personal meditation with no time constraints, I will use the longer version. Following is the English translation of the Beauty Prayer in its entirety:

*In beauty I walk*

*With beauty before me I walk*

*With beauty behind me I walk*

*With beauty above me I walk*

*With beauty around me I walk*

*It has become beauty again*

*It has become beauty again*

*It has become beauty again*

*It has become beauty again*

The Beauty Prayer word code is a blueprint for how we can choose to see beauty in everyday life. The application is clear. The instructions are precise. In our high-tech era of Internet connectivity and miniaturized circuits that fit onto a credit card chip, it may be easy to overlook the power that choice brings to our lives. Within the quantum understanding of a world where our inner beliefs become our outer world, what technology could be simpler or more powerful than the power of choice?

## HOW TO USE WISDOM CODE 12

The power of wisdom codes comes from their repetition and doing so in the affirmative. This imprints a code on the subconscious mind. When we create heart/brain harmony, as described in "How to Use the Wisdom Codes" (see page xix), we open a "hotline" to communicate directly with the subconscious mind.

From a place of heart/brain harmony, recite this code silently, or out loud, from the version that you are most drawn to, until you feel a shift toward greater strength and harmony regarding your choices in life. For the Abbreviated and Informal English Translation, the word *you* may be replaced with *I* to make the prayer more personal. The key is to embrace this code with a focus of awareness, breath, and feeling in the heart rather than the mind. For your convenience, I'm including multiple versions of the Beauty Prayer.

### Abbreviated and Informal English Translation

*The beauty that you live with*

*The beauty that you live by*

*The beauty upon which you base your life*

### Abbreviated and Informal Navajo Translation

*Nizhonigoo bil iina*

### Complete and Formal English Translation

*In beauty I walk*

*With beauty before me I walk*

*With beauty behind me I walk*

*With beauty above me I walk*

*With beauty around me I walk*

*It has become beauty again*

*It has become beauty again*

*It has become beauty again*

*It has become beauty again*

**Complete and Formal Navajo**

*Hózhóogo náashaa doo*

*Shitsiji' hózhóogo náashaa doo*

*Shikeedee hózhóogo náashaa doo*

*Shideigi hózhóogoo náashaa doo*

*T'áá altso shinaagóó hózhóogo náashaa doo*

*Hózhó náhásdlii'*

*Hózhó náhásdlii'*

*Hózhó náhásdlii'*

*Hózhó náhásdlii'*

# Notes

# wisdom code 13

## Vedic Mantra

WISDOM CODE 13: Om Namah Shivaya.

USE: This code is a traditional Hindu mantra that awakens our self-confidence to find strength and purpose in life.

SOURCE: The Yajurveda, Vedic text

The effects and benefits of chanting ancient Hindu mantras are well documented in the scientific literature. A 2002 report published in the *Corsini Encyclopedia of Psychology and Behavioral Science* stated that the physiological benefits of repeating mantras include "lowered levels of tension, slower heart rate, decreased blood pressure, lower oxygen consumption, and increased alpha wave production."

And while these powerful sound/word/cell relationships may appear as new discoveries to some modern scientists, in ancient Hindu traditions the use of spoken mantras has long been known to have powerful effects upon the body, as well as the mind. Before his death in 2010, the Vedic scholar Thomas Ashley-Farrand stated: "Mantras have a very specific effect on our mental, emotional, physical and spiritual states. Indian sages teach that these sound meditations can actually have the power to transform our human conditions, including relationships, health, happiness, career, finances, and success, to name a few."

Considering the ancient traditions, as well as the modern research, it should come as no surprise that the use of mantras extends to the deepest levels of the human psyche, as well as being reflected in the emotions and vital signs of the body.

## THE HINDU MANTRA OF STRENGTH

One of the most widely used of the Hindu chants is the ancient mantra of strength, *Om Namah Shivaya*. This mantra originated as one of the 1,800 hymns preserved in the Vedic texts as the Yajurveda and honors Shiva, one of the three primary deities in the Hindu tradition.

Working in concert with Brahma, the creator, and Vishnu, the preserver, Shiva provides a powerful harmony between these primal forces in a way that is often referred to as the *destroyer*. It's because of this interpretation that the mere mention of Shiva's name often evokes a sense of death and destruction.

Perhaps one of the best-known observations of this correlation was the reaction of Robert Oppenheimer as he witnessed the detonation of the first atomic bomb in a test on July 16, 1945. Known as the father of the atomic bomb, Oppenheimer, who was also an avid reader of the classic from Hindu literature the Mahabharata, famously spoke the words of Lord Shiva from the text, "Now I am become death, the destroyer of worlds."

In 2017, I had the opportunity to visit to the world's largest and most complex machine, the CERN Large Hadron Collider that straddles the border between France and Switzerland. It was during my visit that I discovered why the destruction associated with Shiva is only a part of the story. Formally known as the European Organization for Nuclear Research (or Conseil Européen pour la Recherche Nucléaire in French), the CERN physics laboratory represents one of the largest cooperative scientific efforts in the history of the world. The goal of the facility is to provide the advanced technology to explore the laws of physics that emerged immediately after the universe formed. During my visit to CERN, I was fascinated to discover that the gift that India presented to the laboratory had nothing to do with advanced technology— at least in the traditional sense.

Towering over me in a courtyard between two buildings was a large-scale sculpture of the dancing form of Shiva known as the *Nataraja*, which may be translated to "lord of the dance." The meaning of this particular form of Shiva is the reason I'm describing it here. While it's true that Shiva is frequently described as the destroyer, a deeper exploration of Hindu tradition reveals that the name is often appended with the name *transformer* as well. And while the qualities, destruction and transformation, are often used interchangeably, it may be more accurate to describe them as part of a sequence rather than substitutes for one another.

The reason is simple. For something to become transformed, it is sometimes necessary to replace what exists with a new, hopefully greater expression of itself. In doing so, the old version must be destroyed to make way for the birth of the new. So, in this sense, while Shiva may appear to destroy what exists in the present, destruction is not the goal. Rather it is a stepping-stone toward the revelation of what emerges from the destruction.

This distinction is the reason that the Indian government chose Shiva over the other deities to present to CERN. The advanced experiments in physics done there are designed to reveal the deepest truths of our existence. To arrive at this new understanding and reveal creation's secrets, it is necessary to destroy subatomic particles by means of high-speed collisions.

This distinction is also the reason that the mantra Om Namayah Shivaya can be such a powerful wisdom code for our lives. By invoking the power of Shiva in our lives, we destroy our old ideas of self-limitation and free ourselves to transform into new expressions of ourselves that embody our deepest strengths.

## THE MEANING OF THE MANTRA

The ancient chant Om Namah Shivaya remains as one of the most widely used of the Vedic mantras today—which is both chanted and sung by people around the world. Its longevity is attributed to its simplicity, as well as its universality. As we've seen with other ancient languages, there is no one-to-one correspondence between ancient Sanskrit and modern English words. For this reason, any translation is only an approximation of the original meaning.

The following descriptions can help us to understand the intent of what we're saying as we recite this ancient chant for inner strength.

## Om

The original vibration that existed before the birth of the universe. As such, this primal sound simultaneously represents the pure existence of everything, and nothing.

## Namah

This word means "to adorn" or "to bow in adoration." Within the context of this mantra, it is a statement of honoring the transformation of our perceptions from learned feelings of inadequacy to the deep truth of our inner strength.

## Shivaya

A form of Shiva meaning "the inner self." We each possess the three faces of the Hindu trilogy: Brahma, the creator; Vishnu, the preserver; and Shiva, the destroyer/transformer. In this mantra, we call upon our inner Shiva—that part of ourselves that has the power to transform our lives.

Taken together, the elements of this ancient, eloquent, and simple wisdom code become an invitation from us, directed to ourselves. In this invitation, we acknowledge three attributes of our being:

- The existence of our inner strength
- Our courage to bring into our lives the strength that already exists
- The power to use our strength to follow through with the choices of transformation we make in our lives

## HOW TO USE WISDOM CODE 13

The power of wisdom codes comes from their repetition and doing so in the affirmative. This imprints a code on the subconscious mind. When we create heart/brain harmony, as described in "How to Use the Wisdom Codes" (see page xix), we open a "hotline" to communicate directly with the sub-conscious mind.

From a place of heart/brain harmony, recite or chant this code silently, or out loud, until you feel the shift in your inner strength to transform your choices and your life. The key is to embrace this code with a focus of awareness, breath, and feeling in the heart rather than the mind.

- *Om Namah Shivaya*
- *Om Namah Shivaya*
- *Om Namah Shivaya*

# Notes

_____

_____

_____

_____

_____

_____

_____

_____

_____

_____

_____

_____

_____

_____

# Notes

_____

_____

_____

_____

_____

_____

_____

_____

_____

_____

_____

_____

_____

# wisdom code 14

## Psalm 23

WISDOM CODE 14: The Lord is my shepherd, I lack nothing. He makes me lie down in green pastures, he leads me beside quiet waters, he refreshes my soul. He guides me along the right paths for his name's sake.

USE: The words of this powerful psalm have endured through the centuries as a source of strength and comfort in times of loss, grief, and need.

SOURCE: The Bible, New International Version, Psalm 23, abbreviated version

One of the most universally recognized, and most commonly recited, hymns from the Christian Bible is Psalm 23, often referred to by the name that reflects the first phrase of the hymn, "The Lord is my shepherd." This psalm is commonly used at funeral and memorial services to comfort those mourning the loss of loved ones. A closer look at the way the psalm is constructed, and the words themselves, reveals why this prayer stands out among the 150 hymns of the book of Psalms.

## PSALM 23: REINTERPRETED

Psalm 23 was composed by the biblical King David during a time in his early life when he was a shepherd tending to his flock of sheep. I mention this because it's through the eyes of a sheepherder caring for and responsible for his flock that the imagery of this psalm is conveyed. And in doing so, it touches something deep and ancient in our psyche. The sense of comfort emerges immediately with the first sentence, "The Lord is my shepherd." A shepherd's job is to watch over, to care for, and to provide for the creatures that depend upon him for their lives and well-being. When we lose a loved one, thinking of God as a shepherd fulfilling this role gives us a sense that our loved one continues to be cared for in their journey to the afterlife. It also gives us a sense that we continue to be cared for in the absence of our loved one.

The powerful imagery of God as a shepherd predates Psalm 23, which is believed to have been composed approximately 3,000 years ago and can be traced back to the time of ancient Babylon. In the text known as the Code of Hammurabi, which was etched into a black rock pillar—a stele— that stood in the center of Hammurabi's city 700 years before the time of David, the 282 rules of conduct given by the

Mesopotamian king conclude with the ancient metaphor of the shepherd, stating: "I am the shepherd who brings well-being and abundant prosperity; my rule is just . . . so that the strong might not oppress the weak, and that even the orphan and the widow might be treated with justice." Clearly, the feeling that we are watched over, and cared for, has held a revered place in the human psyche.

## A Sunday Surprise

One Sunday afternoon there was an unexpected knock at my door. It was especially unexpected because my home at the time was in a secluded area of northern New Mexico, at the end of a dead-end dirt road, an hour from the nearest grocery store and nearly 20 acres from my nearest neighbor. Who could possibly be paying me a visit in the middle of nowhere on a Sunday afternoon? The mystery was quickly solved as I peeked through the partially opened door.

Standing on my porch were two conservatively dressed women holding brochures from the Kingdom Hall of the Jehovah's Witnesses congregation located in the nearest town, 20 miles away. After a few seconds of small talk, they got to the point of their visit.

"We don't mean to disturb you," one of the women said, "but we're wondering if you'd like to talk with us today about the Bible?" They obviously had no way of knowing that as a writer of science and spirituality, one of my great passions was researching the discoveries, as well as the translations, of ancient biblical texts. They were more than surprised at my enthusiastic answer as a big smile came across my face.

"Sure!" I said. "You bet! I'd *love* to talk with you about the Bible. Please come in. Which one would you like to talk about first?"

Their faces went blank as my words echoed across the entryway.

"What do you mean?" they asked. "There's only one Bible."

"Well," I said, "this is where things can get really interesting. There are actually many bibles, and many translations of the many bibles, that are available to scholars today."

"Really?" they replied. "Why don't we know about those?"

Their answer set the stage for the conversation that continued for the next three hours. The theme of the conversation that I had on that day also sets the stage for the solution to the lingering mysteries of the Bible's most cherished verses, including Psalm 23.

## MANY BIBLES, DIFFERENT TRANSLATIONS

The conversation that I had with the ladies mentioned previously began with me sharing a sampling of the bibles and translations that are available to scholars today. The partial list that follows gives us a sense of just how many versions exist today.

King James Version (1611, revised 1769)

American Standard Version (1901)

Thompson Chain Reference Bible (1908)

A New Translation of the Bible (1928)

The Bible: An American Translation (1935)

Knox Bible (1949)

Revised Standard Version (1952)

The Berkeley Version in Modern English (1959)

Dake Annotated Reference Bible (1963)

The Jerusalem Bible (1966)

New American Bible (1970)

New English Bible (1970)

New American Standard Bible (1971)

New King James Version (1982)

Revised English Bible (1989)

New Revised Standard Version (1990)

21st Century King James Version (1994)

Contemporary English Version (1995)

New Living Translation (1996, revised 2004)

New English Translation (2005)

With so many translations and interpretations of the most sacred text of the Christian tradition, the obvious question is, which one is the best? Which version most accurately reflects the original words and intent of the various authors, including Psalm 23? The answer to this question is based upon the preference of the reader and how the text is to be used. For the purpose of the Wisdom Codes, my preferred go-to versions of the Christian Bible are the 1982 New King James Version (KJV) and the 1978 New International Version (NIV). The NIV rendition of the biblical texts draws upon 20th-century technology to reconstruct ancient Aramaic, Hebrew, and Greek biblical texts that include the Masoretic Hebrew text, the Dead Sea Scrolls, the Samaritan Pentateuch, the Latin Vulgate, the Syriac Peshitta, the Aramaic Targum, and the Juxta Hebraica of Jerome for the Psalms.

## SHINING A NEW LIGHT ON PSALM 23

Recognizing that there are numerous translations for the same ideas is important for understanding Psalm 23 because of the nuances that are revealed in the texts. For example, the common King James version begins in verse 1 with the words "The Lord is my shepherd; I shall not want." A common interpretation of this statement is to read it as a command. When we read that we "shall not want," we have a sense that it's *because* we are in the capable hands of our shepherd, that we shouldn't—we "shall not"—want for anything.

In other words, to do so would be to discount the magnitude and capability of our shepherd, the Lord.

The NIV translation, however, based upon the most accurate translations of the original texts, offers us a powerful nuance not found in the common translation. This newer translation reads, "The Lord is my shepherd, I lack nothing."

This translation reads as something more than a command that is to be followed. It reveals the declaration of a possibility regarding our present state of existence. Due to the Lord's role as our shepherd, and to his fulfillment of that role, our present state of being is without want—we have someone watching over us who provides what we need when it comes to the basics of life.

This interpretation is further supported in the itemized list of how our needs are fulfilled. Our shepherd provides our world with food in verse 2 (green pastures were the source of food for David's sheep), restoration and guidance in verse 3, protection in verse 4, strength as we face life's challenges in verse 5, and eternal love and life in verse 6. With these interpretations in mind, it becomes apparent why Psalm 23 is a hymn of strength, as well as comfort.

## HOW TO USE WISDOM CODE 14

Following is the complete text for Psalm 23 as translated in the *New International Version* of the Bible. Recite this code silently in sets of three repetitions, silently or out loud, until you feel the shift of your inner strength replace the doubt of your ability to transform your choices and your life.

- *The Lord is my shepherd, I lack nothing.*

- *He makes me lie down in green pastures, he leads me beside quiet waters,*

- *he refreshes my soul. He guides me along the right paths for his name's sake.*

- *Even though I walk through the darkest valley, I will fear no evil, for you are with me; your rod and your staff, they comfort me.*

- *You prepare a table before me in the presence of my enemies. You anoint my head with oil; my cup overflows.*

- *Surely your goodness and love will follow me all the days of my life, and I will dwell in the house of the Lord forever.*

# Notes

_____

_____

_____

_____

_____

_____

_____

_____

_____

_____

_____

_____

# PART FIVE

# love

*Strive to make your love greater than your need*
*and let love be the most powerful force in your life.*
*Then nothing can overcome you.*

— KATE MCGAHAN,
**HOSPICE COUNSELOR AND SOCIAL WORKER**

The human experience of love is described in many ways, and in many places, throughout history. It's typically described, however, as the loss of romantic love, the yearning to recapture a romantic love that's been lost, or a search for the redemption that love makes possible. So, while descriptions of such experiences are plentiful, the perspective that sees love as a primal force that can preserve or destroy our lives is less so. Throughout my adult life, I've found myself returning time and again to the words that are preserved in the Gospel of Thomas to remind myself of love's power as a force that I already possess. For this reason, rather than dilute this section with additional wisdom codes approximating this potential, I've chosen to explore the power of love as a single, potent offering that was spoken over 2,000 years ago. I've yet to find an additional wisdom code to match the eloquence, simplicity, and directness of these few, powerful words.

## THE CHOICE OF LOVE

Whether we're dealing with the shared tragedy of world events, such as America's September 11, 2001, or the personal tragedy of loss, the role that we allow love to play in our lives is a choice that we'll make at some point. And while the emotional pain and trauma that results from our losses is universal, the way we address our pain is not.

If we allow the hurt of our trauma to linger unresolved, that hurt can destroy us. It can destroy our health, our relationships, and, in so many ways, our lives. If, on the other hand, we can find the strength to love in the presence of our deepest hurts, we can give new meaning to life's most painful experiences. In doing so, we become better versions of ourselves. We are more healed, more present for our families, and stronger members of our communities. It's all about the choice we make to love in the presence of our hurt.

## THE PRICE OF LOVE

The power of love to heal, to free us from the burden of hate, and to catapult us beyond our suffering is a theme that has been recognized, analyzed, and shared by the learned masters of the past. The 13th-century Sufi poet Jalāl ad-Dīn ar-Rūmī, known simply as Rumi, beautifully summarized our relationship to this universal force:

*Your task is not to seek for love,*

*but merely to seek and find*

*all the barriers within yourself*

*that you have built against it.*

In these eloquent yet simple words, Rumi reminds us that we already have love, and love's power, within us. Rather than being something that we must search for, locate, and then strive to assimilate into our existence, love is already within us—we're born with love. Our job is to discover everything about ourselves that is *not* love—the relationship walls, emotional blocks, and psychological dams that keep us from accessing our love. When we dissolve these barriers, love is all that remains.

The more we allow love to heal the hurt in our lives, the more we discover the depth of our capacity to love ourselves, as well as other people.

Eleven centuries before the time of Rumi, the power of love was described by another author in compelling and unmistakable terms using words that are as meaningful today as they were at the time of their writing. Among the ancient Gnostic texts that were discovered with the Nag Hammadi Library are passages suggesting that our vulnerability to suffering is the mystical doorway to healing and life. In the Gospel of Thomas, for example, the author describes the power of love as part of a discourse from the master teacher Jesus: "Blessed is the man who has suffered, and found life."

In another portion of the same teaching, Jesus states: "That which you have will save you if you bring it forth from yourselves." In this single, concise, and powerful statement, we are reminded that our love is the source of all healing that we may experience. The key, however, is this: *to feel our love, we must be vulnerable to our pain.* It's through the depth of our hurt that we discover how deeply we can feel. And as we allow ourselves to feel, rather than trying to mask or deny our feelings, we discover our capacity for love.

Simply put, hurt is the price that we sometimes pay to discover that we already have the love we need to heal ourselves. Sometimes, merely knowing of the relationship between wisdom, hurt, and love is enough to catapult us from the pain at one end of our emotional spectrum to the healing that awaits at the other end of the spectrum.

## LOVE AS FORGIVENESS

Almost universally, the power of forgiveness has been acknowledged throughout time and across cultures and continents. American writer Ernest Holmes described this power beautifully when he said, "Through the power of love, we can let go of past history and begin again." Here we're reminded that in the depths of our love, and the forgiveness that our love makes possible, is the key to move forward from the emotional burden and atrocities of the past. This is true for individuals and families. It's also true for societies and entire nations. The reason is because what has happened in the past is part of our history today. And unless we discover a way to go backward in time to right the wrongs, and undo the horrors, of the past, our personal and collective history will remain an unalterable part of our memory.

Just to be clear, for the purpose of this discussion, the act of forgiveness is being treated as a personal act that is intended for personal healing. As described beautifully by Andrea Brandt, Ph.D., forgiveness doesn't excuse what another person has done; it doesn't mean that you need to tell another person that he or she is forgiven; it doesn't mean that you should forget what has happened or should not continue to have strong feelings about a violation of trust or a physical or emotional boundary. And perhaps most importantly, forgiveness isn't for the person that you are forgiving. It's for you. Forgiveness is an act of love that you perform for yourself.

Brandt describes forgiveness beautifully, stating, "By forgiving, you are accepting the reality of what happened and finding a way to live in a state of resolution with it."

# wisdom code 15

## Gospel of Thomas

WISDOM CODE 15: If you bring forth what is within you, what you bring forth will save you. If you do not bring forth what is within you, what you do not bring forth will destroy you.

USE: A reminder that we harbor a force within us whose expression has the power to heal us, yet whose repression has the power to destroy us.

SOURCE: The Gospel of Thomas, discovered in its complete form as part of Egypt's Nag Hammadi Library in 1945

The power of forgiveness is more than an academic exercise. It's real. And it's a power that has been proven time and again in the real world. The choice to love, and the forgiveness that is possible from love, is a common thread that weaves its way through the lives of those who have survived *and transcended* history's atrocities. From today's survivors of unspeakable horrors endured in the Nazi death camps between 1933 and 1945 to hostage negotiator Terry Waite's living 1,763 days of captivity in the hands of Hezbollah extremists and Alison Botha's miraculous survival following being left for dead after the brutal attack that is the subject of the 2016 documentary simply titled *Alison*, forgiveness is the key that has empowered these people, and others, to move forward with their lives after enduring horrors.

## BEYOND THEORY: FORGIVENESS IN ACTION

Eva Mozes Kor, who died at the age of 85, endured atrocities that were performed under the guise of medical experimentation at the Auschwitz concentration/labor/death camp until she was freed at the end of the Second World War. Before her death in 2019, she returned to Auschwitz to accompany an educational group. What made Eva's visit so exceptional, however, is that in addition to the tour group, she was accompanied by one of the Nazi doctors who had performed the horrific experiments on her. At a memorial service to honor those who died at the camp, she forgave him for the role he played in the atrocities, as well as for the suffering she and her twin sister had endured as a result of what he'd done.

She later shared her experience in an interview published by the popular Tel Aviv newspaper *Yedioth Ahronoth*: "I forgive them for killing my parents, for robbing me of the rest of my family, for taking my childhood from me, for turning my life into hell, for creating nightmares that accompanied me every night in the past 60 years. In my name—and only in my name—I forgive them for all those horrific acts." Kor described how her life changed in the presence of her forgiveness, stating, "As I did that [the act of forgiveness], I felt a burden of pain was lifted from me. I was no longer in the grip of pain and hate." Leaving no doubt about the power of her forgiveness and the role it has played in her life, she clarified, "I was finally free."

In this poignant example of seemingly unforgivable cruelty, we see the power that is described in the Gospel of Thomas. By choosing to bring forth the love and subsequent forgiveness within her, Eva Kor transcended the emotional suffering and the biological consequences of illness and disease that typically accompany prolonged and unresolved anger. In doing so, she lived to an age that is considered advanced even by today's standards—85 years—where the life expectancy for a woman in the United States averages 80 years. If Eva had chosen to cling to her anger, and to dwell upon the horrors of her experience, the science of epigenetics shows that in all probability, the consequence of such a choice would have led to compromises in her immune system, her cardiovascular system, and her body's mechanisms of DNA and cell integrity. In other words, there is a greater probability that her failure to bring forth what was within her—love and love's power to forgive—would have destroyed her.

## DISTORTED LOVE

The beauty of love's power is that it's not limited to a select group of people who have a rare skill or knowledge of an esoteric principle that sets them apart from their family, friends, and neighbors. The ability to love is universal. Our ability to give and to receive love is a primal capacity that lives within each of us. For some of us, the knowledge of our capacity is close to the surface, and we've been blessed to recognize it early in life, and we love willingly and easily. Love is a cornerstone in our existence. More commonly, however, our capacity to love is not so easy to embrace. It's hidden, and we're the ones who have hidden it.

From the time of our childhood and through our experiences in life, we've often felt—*we've perceived*—that it's not safe to reveal our love in the world. In light of this perception, we've expertly masked this primal capacity from our family, our friends, and those closest to us. Without the benefit of this original code, we go through life with a distorted view of our relationship to the world, other people, and ultimately, to ourselves. The difference between our primal capacity to love and the perceptions of love that we hold today is the distortion that brings us suffering, disappointment, and fear. The emotional equation for our distortions may be thought of as the following formula:

(Original Capacity to Love) – (Today's Perception of Love) = A Distortion That Appears as Suffering

For some people, the present-day perception of a life-event—the hurt, loss, or betrayal by our loved ones—has become so painful that the distortion is unbearable. Skillfully and masterfully, these powerful individuals create behavior patterns that allow them to get through life with less pain and survive their distorted thinking. The reality, however, is that the behavior that gets them through often replaces one painful distortion for another. We know these repetitive patterns of pain as addictions.

## ADDICTION: DISTORTED LOVE

For the purpose of this discussion, addiction may be defined as a repeating pattern of behavior that you give priority to and rearrange the rest of your life to accommodate. The word *addiction* is often associated with substance abuse of chemicals, drugs, and alcohol. And while these are certainly common expressions of behavior patterns that people will rearrange their lives to accommodate, there are others that are not so obvious. These often subtle patterns may be masked as socially acceptable patterns of lifestyle and include, but are not limited to, intimate relationships, the chronic quest for power, needless spending of money, the chronic quest for control, living in lack, the chronic need to work to make money, the chronic obsession with sex, and chronic illness.

Each of these terms describes a pattern in which people have shifted the priorities in their lives and made room for a certain focus by sacrificing time with their families and loved ones. The jewel that is present in the abyss of addiction is that the consequences that are suffered do not happen overnight. They unfold gradually over a period of time. And in doing so, we are given ample opportunities to recognize and heal the thinking underlying the addiction. By personalizing Wisdom Code 15, we give ourselves a powerful tool to do just that.

## OUR PERSONAL WISDOM CODE

Jesus revealed Wisdom Code 15 to his followers, as well as future generations, as the single most potent and powerful key to heal our lives and transcend our suffering. The good news is that it's a power that we already have. It's not something that we need to go into the world to discover. It's not "out there" in the world around us or something that we need to construct. It already lives within each of us. It's love.

When we heal the distorted perceptions at the root of our suffering, all that remains is our love.

### The Original Generalized Template

*If you bring forth what is within you, what you bring forth will save you.*

*If you do not bring forth what is within you, what you do not bring forth will destroy you.*

We also can take the ancient template describing the power of our love in Wisdom Code 15 and restate it in the first person. In doing so, we create a personal mantra to remind us of the love that we're born with and its power in our lives. And due to contemporary research in neuroscience, we know that the effectiveness of a mantra comes from the repetition of the code to the subconscious mind and doing so in the affirmative. For this reason, there is no need to recite the consequences of *not* bringing forth what is within us. Rather we state the benefit as follows:

### The Personal Mantra Stated in the Affirmative

*If I bring forth what is within me, what I bring forth will save me.*

In the presence of this honest assessment of love's power, the key is to consider the object of our forgiveness from the objectivity of the heart, rather than the polarity of the brain.

## HOW TO USE WISDOM CODE 15

When we create heart/brain harmony (as described in "How to Use the Wisdom Codes" (see page xix), we open a "hotline" to communicate directly with the subconscious mind. From a place of heart/brain harmony, recite the code repeatedly, until you feel an empowered shift in your ability to love that may take the form of peace acceptance in your inner state. The key is to embrace this code with a focus of awareness, breath, and feeling in the heart rather than the mind.

*If I bring forth what is within me, what I bring forth will save me.*

## Notes

_____

_____

_____

_____

_____

_____

_____

_____

_____

_____

_____

_____

_____

# PART SIX

# the power codes

*Words are singularly the most powerful*
*force available to humanity.*

—Yehuda Berg, rabbi

# power code 1

## I Will

POWER CODE 1: I will.

USE: This ancient code affirms to our body and declares to the universe that we are empowered to choose an outcome.

SOURCE: The Bible, King James Version, book of Matthew, chapter 8, verses 2–3

The best science of the 20th and 21st centuries suggests
that we are much more than simple observers living a
brief moment of time in a creation that is separate from us.
From the paradigm-altering twin photon experiments that
revealed the phenomenon of entanglement in 1997, to the
discovery of the universal Higgs field announced by CERN
scientists in 2012, modern science is catching up with the
intuitive wisdom of 5,000 years of indigenous and spiritual
traditions. It's now an accepted fact that there is an underlying field of energy that coalesced within the first fraction of a
second when the universe began. The computer models, the
mathematic equations, and now the small-scale laboratory
re-creations of this primal event confirm that everything we
know and experience in our world is made of tiny packets
of energy—*quanta*—that constantly emerge from, and are
reabsorbed into, this all-pervading field of energy. The field
is identified by names that range from the Matrix, the Prime
Source, and the Divine Matrix to simply the Field, as well
as others. Perhaps it's no coincidence that the scientific description of this energy closely parallels the same principles
described by the wisdom traditions of the past.

From the ancient Indian Vedas, believed by some scholars
to date to 5000 B.C.E., to the 2,000-year-old Dead Sea Scrolls,
a general theme seems to suggest that the world is actually the
mirror of things that are happening in a realm that we cannot
see from our vantage point in time and space. Nonetheless,
the realm is real and we're part of it. We're interacting with it
in each moment of every day. From this perspective, our intimate relationships, friendships, state of health, successes, and
failures are all reflections of ongoing relationships that are
occurring in the unseen realm of this field. Commenting on
fragments of the Dead Sea Scroll known as the Songs of the
Sabbath Sacrifice, scholars summarize the content, stating

that they imply, "What happens on earth is but a pale reflection of that greater, ultimate reality."

## ARE WE OBSERVERS OR CREATORS?

The nature of the Field, and our relationship to it, is the source of an emotional and often heated debate among scientific minds that began in the 19th century and continues today. While the technical arguments for the controversy are complex, the reason for the debate is simple. If there is, in fact, an invisible realm of existence that is the source of our everyday experiences, and if we have the ability to access this realm to change what ultimately happens in our lives, it changes everything we've been led to believe about ourselves and our world. And in that change, we are empowered to participate in the outcome of the things that matter most to us in life.

In a quote from his autobiographical notes, Albert Einstein shared his deeply held belief that we are separate from the everyday world and live as passive observers that have very little influence upon the world around us. "Out yonder there was this huge world," he said, "which exists independently of us human beings and which stands before us like a great, eternal riddle, at least partially accessible to our inspection and thinking."

In contrast to Einstein's view, which is still widely held by many scientists today, the Professor John Wheeler, a Princeton physicist and colleague of Einstein, offered a radically different perspective of our role in creation. In terms that are bold, clear, and graphic, Wheeler said, "We had this old idea, that there is a universe *out there*, and here is man, the observer, safely protected from the universe by a six-inch slab of plate glass." In other words, he was acknowledging the perspective that Einstein held of us separated from the world around us. That perspective changed quickly, however, with a series of paradigm-shattering experiments that demonstrated we're not as separate from the world as once believed. These revelations include the still-controversial double-slit experiment that reveals how electrons change from particles into waves of energy just from the act of being observed— because someone is looking at them. Referring to this kind of experiment, Wheeler continues, "Now we learn from the quantum world that even to observe so minuscule an object as an electron we have to shatter the plate glass; we have to reach in there. . . . So the old word *observer* simply has to be crossed off the books, and we must put in the new word *participator*."

## CONSCIOUSNESS CREATES!

What a shift! In a radically different interpretation of our relationship to our bodies and the world around us, Wheeler is stating that it's impossible for us simply to watch the world happen around us. From his interpretation of the data, he's telling us that we're changemakers. Sometimes consciously and sometimes subconsciously, we're constantly participating in the outcome of the things that happen in our lives, and in our world.

Experiments in quantum physics do show, in fact, that the act of us looking at something as tiny as an electron—just focusing our awareness upon what that electron is doing for even an instant in time—changes its properties during the time we are looking. The experiments suggest that the very act of observation is an act of creation, and that consciousness is doing the creating. These findings seem to support Wheeler's statement that we can no longer think of ourselves merely as onlookers who have no effect on the world that we are observing.

When we look at the everyday expression of our spiritual and material abundance, our relationships, careers, and physical health, our deepest loves and greatest achievements, as well as our fears and the lack of all of these things, we may, in fact, be looking squarely at the mirror of our truest and sometimes most unconscious beliefs. We see them in our surroundings because they are made manifest through a Field of energy that exists everywhere, at all times, and connects all things.

## WE ARE THE ARTISTS AS WELL AS THE ART

We are the Field. The atoms of our physical bodies are constantly appearing and disappearing, emerging and collapsing, following the blueprint of our consciousness to produce the selves that we are familiar with. In other words, we are like artists expressing our deepest passions, fears, and desires through the living essence of a mysterious quantum canvas. But unlike a conventional artist's canvas, which exists in one place at a given time, our canvas is the same stuff that everything else is made of. It exists everywhere. It's always present.

And while artists are traditionally thought of as separate from their artwork, within the Field the separation between art and artist disappears. We *are* the canvas as well as the images upon the canvas. We *are* the tools as well as the artists using the tools. Just as artists work and refine an image until it's just right in their minds, we appear to do the same thing with the relationships in our lives. Through our palette of beliefs, judgments, and emotions, we experience the relationships that allow us to perfect our canvas of life. Just the way an artist uses the same canvas again and again while searching for the perfect expression of an idea, we may think of ourselves as perpetual artists, building a creation that is ever changing and never ending.

The implications of being surrounded by a malleable world of our own making are vast, powerful, and, to some people, maybe a little frightening. Our ability to use the Field intentionally and creatively suddenly empowers us to change everything about the way we see our role in the universe. At the very least, it suggests that there is much more to life than chance happenings and occasional synchronicities that we deal with the best we can.

Ultimately, our relationship to the quantum essence that connects us to everything else reminds us that we are creators ourselves. As creators, we may express our deepest desires of healing, abundance, joy, and peace in everything from our bodies and our lives to our relationships. And we may do so consciously in the time and manner that we choose.

## WRINKLES IN THE FIELD

From a quantum way of viewing the world, everything we experience may be thought of as "wrinkles" disturbing an otherwise harmonious Field of energy. It may be no coincidence that ancient spiritual and poetic traditions describe our existence in much the same way. The Vedic traditions, for example, describe a unified field of "pure consciousness" that bathes and permeates all of creation. In these traditions, our experiences of thought, feeling, and emotion and the fear and judgment they create are viewed as disturbances—interruptions in a field that is otherwise smooth and motionless.

In a similar fashion, the 5th century "Hsin-Hsin Ming" (a title that translates to "Faith Mind Verses") describes the properties of an essence that is the blueprint for everything in creation. It's called the Tao, and just as we see in the Vedic scriptures, it's ultimately beyond description. The Tao is all that is. It's the container of all experience, as well as the experience itself. The Tao is described as perfect, "like vast space where nothing is lacking, and nothing is in excess."

According to the Hsin-Hsin Ming, it is only when we disturb the tranquility of the Tao through our judgments that its harmony eludes us. When the inevitable does happen, and we find ourselves enmeshed in feelings of anger and separation, the text offers guidelines to remedy this condition.

> *To come directly into harmony with this reality just simply say when doubt arises, "Not two." In this "not two" nothing is separate, nothing is excluded.*

I admit that while thinking of ourselves as a disturbance in the Field may take some of the romance out of life, it also gives us a powerful way to think of our world and ourselves. If we want to create new, healthy, and life-affirming relationships, bring healing romance into our lives, or bring a peaceful solution to the world's problems, for example, we must create a new disturbance in the Field, one that mirrors our desire. We must create a new wrinkle in the stuff that space, time, our bodies, and the world are made of.

## THE USE AND POWER OF *WILL*

We commonly use the word *will* when we state our intention in the moment to do or say something at a future time. "I *will* take out the trash in the morning" or "I *will* pick up a loaf of bread on my way home from work" are examples of this use of the word. In these statements, using *will* indicates that while we plan to do something, that something is not happening in the present moment. We are stating that it's going to happen at some point in the future that may range from the next minute to hours, days, or even longer from the present moment. We intend for it to happen. And we may be absolutely sincere in our intention. However, stating that we will do something at another time opens the door to procrastination and extenuating circumstances that prevent our intended action from ever happening.

In the biblical traditions we see another way to consider *will*, and the use of the word *will* in our lives. Please note that I'm referencing the biblical texts here as historic records of wisdom, rather than religious texts of doctrine. The New Testament book of Matthew, for example, records a public exchange made between the learned teacher Jesus of Nazareth and a diseased man who approached him asking for healing. In chapter 8, verses 2 and 3, the Gospel describes Jesus's use of Power Code 1—the phrase *I will*—followed by the statement of his intended outcome. The account begins when the man approaches Jesus and says:

> *Lord, if thou wilt, thou canst make me clean.*

This sentence sets the scene for two events to occur:

- It creates the conditions necessary to facilitate healing.
- The man heals.

By asking for help, the man avails himself of the opportunity to receive his personal healing. In other words, he is willing to accept the change that is possible and is stating his acceptance to the universe.

The account then describes both Jesus's physical action and the words that accompany it:

*And Jesus put forth his hand, and touched him, saying I will; be thou clean. And immediately his leprosy was cleansed.*

In this historic account, we are shown a very different use of the concept of personal will or will power. Here we see the use of will to alter an expression of the Field. To be absolutely clear, this is very different from the act of intention. Jesus didn't state that he *intended* to facilitate the sick man's healing at some other time, as would be implied in the traditional use of the word *will*, as a future-tense assertion, "I *will* heal you." Here the word *will* is being used to declare the existence of an outcome that is already present.

*I will* is the declaration.

*Be thou clean* is the outcome.

Through this use of the word *will*, Jesus acknowledges these things:

- The existence of the Field that modern science now confirms is the container for all things that happen in our world
- His present and active relationship to the Field
- The role of his consciousness in modifying the Field through an act of will

Just as we do in a direct affirmation that begins from the outcome, Jesus declares the outcome—*he owns his relationship to the Field*. In making this declaration, the statement that he speaks following the words *I will* becomes real, true, and manifest.

# Notes

_____

_____

_____

_____

_____

_____

_____

_____

_____

_____

_____

_____

_____

# power code 2

## I Am

POWER CODE 2: I am.

USE: This ancient code claims the truth of the moment.

SOURCE: The Bible, book of Exodus, chapter 3, verse 14

The second power code described in the biblical texts begins with Moses's experience on Mount Sinai. As with Jesus's use of the words *I will*, described previously, Power Code 2 is expressed in the eloquent simplicity of two words as well—the words *I am*. The mystery of the meaning of these two words has been the subject of controversy for over two millennia and remains so today.

Both the ancient Hebrew and Christian traditions record two instances when God is said to have revealed his personal name to the people of the earth. Both accounts are preserved in the book of Exodus. And although the Holy Quran also describes the general theme of these ancient accounts, including the act of Moses receiving God's laws upon Mount Sinai, the actual name of God does not appear to be revealed outwardly in the Islamic texts.

In the third chapter of Exodus, God reveals that he is the same God referred to by Moses's ancestors in the past: the god of Abraham, the god of Isaac, and the god of Jacob, as well as the god of Amram, Moses's father. Through a rare and direct communication with God, Moses asks for greater clarity as to precisely who he is speaking with on Mount Sinai so he can answer the questions that are sure to arise when his followers ask him about his encounter.

> *When I come to the Israelites and say to them, "The God your fathers has sent me to you," and they ask me, "What is his name?" what shall I say to them?*

And this is where the mystery of God's answer begins, and the secret of this power code is revealed.

Beginning in Exodus 3:14, God initially answers Moses using three Hebrew words: *Ehyeh Asher Ehyeh*. These words are commonly translated into English as "I Am that I Am."

The source of the mystery, and the controversy, that has lasted for over 3,200 years is in the translation of this simple phrase.

## LOST IN TRANSLATION?

While one school of scholars has traditionally interpreted the initial part of Moses's conversation as the moment that God revealed his name, a closer examination of the Hebrew language offers a deeper understanding of this mysterious phrase.

As we discovered in the chapter on Wisdom Code 2, God's personal name is replaced over 6,800 times in the Hebrew Bible with substitute names. The key here is that while these substitute words represent the various qualities of God's presence, they are *not* his name. The personal name God revealed to Moses in his next sentence is recorded in Exodus 3:15:

> *Thus shalt thou say unto the children of Israel, the Lord God of your fathers, the God of Abraham, the God of Isaac, and the God of Jacob, hath sent me unto you: . . .*

And while scholars typically stop with this identification, what follows leaves no doubt as to what God is revealing to Moses. God concludes his sentence by saying:

> *This is my name for ever, and this is my memorial unto all generations.*

The name that God is referring to here is the coded name underlying the words *the Lord*. In the original Hebrew texts, the name that was replaced is the direct and personal name of God represented as four mysterious Hebrew letters—yod, hey, vav, and hey. These letters are known as the *tetragrammaton* (meaning four-letter word), and when translated, they become *Yahweh* (pronounced "yah way"). This is the name that is so holy, so sacred, and rendered so unspeakable by orthodox followers of the Jewish faith, that it is replaced throughout the Hebrew Bible.

So, we see from these subtle yet critical nuances of translation that *Ehyeh Asher Ehyeh* is not, in fact, God's personal name. Nonetheless it reveals a powerful understanding regarding God's existence in all things. Due to the nature of the Hebrew language, this phrase may be translated variously as "I am *who* I am," "I am *that* I am," and "I am *what* I am," as well as "I *will be* what I *will be*." Scholars generally agree that the most favored translation is the latter: "I will be what I will be."

With this translation in mind, we discover that the "I Am" power code is actually a hidden form of the "I will" power code described previously. As "I am who I am" is also "I will be what I will be," we see the power of the word *will* hidden in *I Am*. By stating "I Am," God is clarifying the nature of his immediate and sustained relationship to the Field.

| Code | Meaning |
|------|---------|
| *I am* | *I claim in the Universal Field that the action following this statement is already manifest in a state of existence.* |
| *that* | *The state of existence is present and sustained.* |
| *I am* | *I claim in the Universal Field that the action following this statement is already manifest in a state of existence.* |

Through the words *I Am that I Am*, Moses is being shown the key to God's relationship with the Field, and how to wield the selfsame power to alter what exists in Field. He is also given the power to access this code in his own life.

Jesus's use of these codes and his revealing their use to his followers makes these codes available to us today. Speaking the words *I Am* from an intentional state of heart/brain coherence, we are given the coded language of this doorway to change. God revealed it. Jesus demonstrated it. And today, we are challenged to use this powerful code to transcend the limiting beliefs that keep us from experiencing the deepest truths of our existence.

## KEYS TO SUCCESSFULLY USING THE POWER CODES

The key to the successful use of both *I will* and *I am* is to do these two things:

1. Be very clear about what you are choosing to will into existence.

2. Be free of judgment and attachment with respect to the outcome.

When we consider what modern science has confirmed about the nature of the Field, and our relationship to it, these two guidelines make perfect sense. The Universal Field does not judge the appropriateness of what we give it to reflect. It doesn't know about the goodness or badness, the rightness or wrongness of what we feed it. It's simply a mirror. And just as the bathroom mirror honestly reflects our appearance when we venture a first look in the morning, the Field honestly reflects the views and beliefs that we hold through our relationships, quality of health, and success in the world.

Once again, a reference from the historic teaching of Jesus preserved in the lost Gospel of Thomas describes this relation and the key to our success in using the quantum mirror in our lives. "When you make the two one," he says, "you will become the sons of man, and when you say, 'Mountain, move away,' it will move away." In this statement, the master is reminding us of the literal nature of the Field.

To optimize our success when it comes to altering the relationships, health, abundance, and success that the Field is reflecting to us, we must be clear on our desired outcome, while at the same time remaining free of our attachment to the outcome. Although at first blush this may sound like a contradiction, when we break down the statements, the reason why to both specify our desire and also detach from it becomes clear.

When we have an attachment to a particular outcome, we can only have that attachment by comparing our experience to something else. And it's through comparison that we fall into the ancient trap of judgment. We tend to hold our experience in the light of what someone else has accomplished and judge our success or failure by making the comparison.

The question that we must ask ourselves is who or what we should use as our point of reference. And if the answer is anything other than our own direct experience, then we are given insight into the source of our judgment. In the absence of comparing our accomplishment of anything in life to another person or event—when we make the two one—all that remains is the effort itself. And if we've truly done the very best that we are capable of in the moment, then we can only be successful. This is the power of Jesus's words regarding making "the two one."

## HOW TO USE THE POWER CODES

Being specific and concise are the keys to any successful conversation with the Universal Field of energy that connects all things. When you are ready to apply either Power Code 1, *"I am,"* or Power Code 2, *"I will,"* to manifest what you want, use to following guidelines to optimize your experience.

Using the steps described in the "How to Use the Wisdom Codes" (see page xix), create coherence between your heart and brain. The key is to do so with a focus of awareness, breath, and feeling in the heart rather than the mind.

Then, from within the place of objective nonattachment created by heart/brain harmony, clearly and concisely, either silently or out loud, say either, "I will," or "I am," followed by the brief and concise declaration of your desired outcome.

- I will _____

- I am _____

Afterward, to the best of your ability, *feel* the feeling of the outcome that you are stating, using as many senses as possible: feel the gratitude and joy of the outcome manifest, hear the sound of your own voice in the presence of your outcome manifest, see the outcome clearly in your mind's eye, and so on.

Close the *I will/I am* code with gratitude, speaking silently or out loud the words *Thank you* directly to the Field, rather than saying, "I give thanks," which would remove you by one step from the gratitude you are expressing.

# Notes

_____

_____

_____

_____

_____

_____

_____

_____

_____

_____

_____

_____

_____

# the parables

*Humans are not ideally set up to understand logic;*
*they are ideally set up to understand stories.*

—ROGER C. SCHANK, COGNITIVE SCIENTIST

The purpose of the wisdom codes in this book is to offer a collection of specific words that have been refined, and standardized, in prayers, mantras, and chants throughout the ages to help us to feel differently about our lives and our world. In addition to the brief words and phrases commonly used in the past, learned masters and great teachers have also used simple stories known as *parables* in a similar way. While the paragraph length of a parable may make it difficult to use as a chant or prayer, the message conveyed by the parable nonetheless has the power to shift our perception of life and the world. In doing so, we are changed in the presence of the parable. For this reason, I've included two parables for this collection of wisdom codes. I hope you appreciate them in your life as much as I have in mine.

## THE POWER OF THE PARABLE

We are a species of stories. We tell ourselves stories for a simple reason—because stories work. Novelist Scott Turow summed up this fact beautifully when he asked, "Who are we . . . but the stories we tell about ourselves, particularly if we accept them?" Our stories help us to make sense of the world, and what we see happening in it. They also help us learn important life lessons and heal life's hurts. Through our stories we also preserve what we learn in a way that can be easily passed to our children and future generations.

We've shared and recorded our stories from the time that the earliest members of our species began to communicate with one another. The Australian aboriginals, for example, boast one of the longest continuous traditions of culture in the world. Scientific analysis confirms that some of their cave paintings date to 28,000 years before the present. Some that were sealed airtight are believed to be even older; they're now estimated to date as far back as 32,000 years ago! From these ancient examples to the modern stories of science that offer more recent explanations for human origins, we've explained the cosmos and our place in it through stories, metaphors, and parables. And while we all enjoy curling up to experience a good story through a book or a film, the reason that we are so drawn to do so appears to come from something more than a desire to be entertained.

New discoveries in psychology and the cognitive sciences suggest that our brains are literally "wired" for stories and storytelling as a way to recall vital information. We recognize this connection intuitively, as it is typically easier to remember the story of relationships between the phases of the moon and fertility, for example—something associated with survival—than it is to remember isolated facts, numbers, and statistics. Cognitive scientist Roger Schank gives us the reason underlying this simple truth, stating: "Humans are not ideally set up to understand logic; they are ideally set up to understand stories." It seems that our neurons are genetically predisposed to "wire and fire" in response to the relationships described in stories rather than isolated data and facts.

As Jonathan Gottschall describes in his book *The Story-telling Animal*, the act of sharing the same story time and again "refines the neural pathways that lead to skillful navigation of life's problems." In other words, it's the act of sharing an idea through the repeated description of a relatable experience that keeps an idea alive and relevant in our community, whether it be an idea of ethics, morality, or cosmology or of simple life skills. The key is that the story illustrates a life situation in a way that helps us to learn from someone else's experience, to heal from an experience, or to avoid the consequences of a difficult situation.

## THE GOSPEL OF THOMAS

Perhaps the best-known of the manuscripts discovered in Nag Hammadi, described previously, in Wisdom Code 15, is the Gospel of Thomas. Also known as the Coptic Gospel of Thomas and by the official name Codex II, the Nag Hammadi Library version of the Gospel of Thomas is the only complete record of this controversial manuscript. It begins with a declaration as to the origin of the 114 sayings and parables that it contains, stating, "These are the hidden words that the living Jesus spoke and Didymus Judas Thomas wrote them down."

Although modern scholars have yet to agree that Didymus Judas Thomas—the biblical apostle Thomas—is actually the author of the document, the words of the manuscript speak for themselves. Through its masterful use of the parables it contains, this scripture gives us powerful insights into the human condition. It depicts the kinds of experiences that are still recognizable in our lives today.

# parable 1

## The Woman and the Jar

PARABLE 1: The parable of the woman and the jar

USE: This key reminds us that our ability to love another person is directly linked to our capacity to love ourselves.

SOURCE: The Gospel of Thomas, discovered in its complete form as part of Egypt's Nag Hammadi Library in 1945

During childhood, we learn to compromise ourselves to survive the challenges of life. Sometimes a compromise can be as simple as a young girl conforming to the desire of her father and brothers to watch a war movie rather than the love story she would have chosen because she's outnumbered by males in the household. A constant pattern of feeling discounted in a family of origin often translates later in life to feeling unheard in the workplace or in friendships and relationships.

Sometimes we compromise something much deeper, such as when we "give in" and agree to do something that our deepest instincts tell us is not right for us. Each time we give in to pressure or temptation we lose something within us—our sense of worth and self-esteem, and our trust in the safety of sharing our opinions and feelings. And while our losses can happen in ways that are socially acceptable, they are nonetheless painful.

Forcing children to take on adult roles and losing their childhood following a family breakup, for example; the loss of racial identity through assimilation as cultures are forced together; and the survival of childhood trauma through repressing emotions of hurt, anger, and loss are among the many ways that we commonly lose these precious pieces of ourselves. Verse 97 of the Gospel of Thomas, the Parable of the Woman and the Jar, is one of the most direct and compelling reminders of the consequences of taking cumulative losses over time. Following is the parable in its entirety.

*The kingdom of the father is like a certain woman who was carrying a jar full of meal. While she was walking on the road, still some distance from home, the handle of the jar broke and the meal emptied out behind her on the road. She did not realize it; she had noticed no incident. When she reached her house, she set the jar down and found it empty.*

## WHAT DOES THIS PARABLE MEAN?

When we take a closer look at the statements that comprise Parable 1, we discover a powerful truth about us and our relationship to love. A statement-by-statement analysis reveals this truth.

### Line 1: The kingdom of the father is like a certain woman who was carrying a jar full of meal.

The human body is often referred to as a vessel, or a jar, in biblical parlance, as we see, for example, in the second book of Timothy: "If a man therefore purge himself from these, he shall be a *vessel* unto honor . . ." (2 Timothy, chapter 2, verse 21).

In Parable 1, the jar that the woman is carrying is us. We are the vessel that holds something of immense value. And just as the woman gradually loses something precious that she was carrying—food for her family—the parable reminds us of how we lose something precious from our vessel as well, often without even knowing it's being lost—our capacity to receive love, as well as to give love, in our lives.

The meal in the jar is our love. It's also the many expressions of love, which include our capacity for compassion and care. As we see in biblical examples, such as the book of Second Corinthians, it's within the vessel of our body that we carry the earthly treasure of our love: "But we have this treasure in earthen vessels, that the excellency of the power may be of God, and not of us" (2 Corinthians, chapter 4, verse 7). Throughout our lives, it's through the different qualities of love that we comfort, nurture, and support others, as well as ourselves, during life's challenges. When we lose the people, places, animals, and things that we hold dear, it's precisely these qualities that give us the strength to survive our loss and get through the experience.

**Line 2: While she was walking on the road, still some distance from home, the handle of the jar broke and the meal emptied out behind her on the road.**

Because we share our love, compassion, and care willingly, these are also the parts of us that are most vulnerable to being lost, innocently given away, or taken from us by those who have power over us. Each time we trust enough to love or nurture someone else and that trust is violated, it's like the handle of the vessel that has broken, allowing the meal of our love to be emptied. We lose a little of ourselves to the experience. Our reluctance to open again to such vulnerability is the way we often learn to survive our deepest hurts and greatest betrayals. It's our mechanism of protection. And each time we reduce our willingness to love by shutting off the access to our truest nature of compassion and nurturing, we are like the meal that is slowly leaving the jar that the woman is carrying.

**Line 3: She did not realize it; she had noticed no incident.**

Little by little, we lose our capacity, and even our willingness, to love. And our loss often occurs without us even realizing that the loss is occurring. The reasons for our loss can be described on a spectrum that ranges from compromising ourselves by "giving in" to unreasonable demands to appease family anger to ensuring our very survival by participating in unhealthy and sometimes even illegal practices to feel safe in a relationship. Sometimes these practices become so routine in our lives that we follow them without acknowledging the

the parables

magnitude of our loss. As in the parable, we don't notice the incidents. We don't notice, that is, until one day we reach into our vessel and discover that it's difficult for us to love another person, because we've lost the foundation of love that we once had for ourselves.

**Line 4: When she reached her house, she set the jar down and found it empty.**

When we find ourselves at a point in life where we find someone we really want to love, someone we really want to open ourselves to and share ourselves with, we reach for love in our vessel, only to find that it is gone. Instead of the love we thought we would find, we discover in its place a reservoir of emptiness. The reason is that we've lost ourselves over time, little by little, to the very experiences that we trusted enough to open to.

## THE GOOD NEWS OF THE WOMAN AND THE JAR

The purpose of this parable is to remind us that our ability to love another person is rooted in our ability to love ourselves. The good news that the master Jesus shared in the subsequent teachings of the Gospel of Thomas is that the parts of us that appear to be absent and the love that seems to have disappeared are never really gone. It is not like they are lost forever. Just as the soul can never be destroyed, our true nature can never be lost. During the times the world seemed to be unsafe, we simply masked these parts of ourselves and hid them away for safekeeping. When we recognize the judgments that lead to the masking of life's deepest hurts, we embark upon a fast path of personal healing. The key to heal our judgments is found in the parables that follow the woman and jar.

In verse 106 of the Gospel of Thomas, Jesus states: "When you make the two one, you will become the sons of man, and when you say, 'Mountain, move away,' it will move away." In other words, it's when we transcend our self-judgment polarities of right and wrong, good and bad, and success and failure that we reclaim the lost parts of ourselves, including our capacity to love (in other words, the meal in our jar) before it slips away from us.

## DISCOVERING IN OTHER PEOPLE WHAT WE'VE LOST IN OURSELVES

The reason that we sometimes betray our beliefs, our love, trust, and compassion, is simple. It's survival. As children we may have discovered that it was easier to remain silent, rather than voicing an opinion at the risk of being ridiculed and invalidated by parents, brothers, sisters, or peers. As the object of abuse in a family, it is much safer to "give in" and forget, rather than to resist those who have power over us. As a society, we accept the killing of others during war, for example, and justify it as a special circumstance for taking a life.

We've all been conditioned to some degree to give ourselves away in the face of conflict, disease, and overwhelming emotion. While we sometimes sacrifice ourselves consciously, more often than not, we do so in ways that we are only now beginning to understand. In each example, we have the opportunity to see a powerful possibility, rather than the judgment of what is right and wrong. For every piece of ourselves that we've given away to be where we find ourselves in life today, there is the emptiness that is left behind. That emptiness is waiting to be filled. And we are constantly searching for whatever it is, and will do whatever it takes, to fill our particular void.

## WHEN OUR JAR IS EMPTY

When we meet a person who has within him or her the very attributes that we have lost, given away, or had taken from us by those who have power over us, the feeling is ecstatic. The person's complementary essence fills our inner void and we say that we feel "whole," "complete." We will do anything to keep that feeling of wholeness alive. This is the key to understanding what happens when we find ourselves mysteriously and magnetically drawn to another person for no obvious reason. When we find our "missing" pieces in others, we will be powerfully and irresistibly drawn to them. We may even believe that we "need" them in our lives, until we remember that what we are so drawn to in them is something that we still have within us. It is simply sleeping. In the awareness that we still have those characteristics and traits, we may unmask them and reincorporate them back into our lives. And when we do, we suddenly find that we are no longer powerfully, magnetically, and inexplicably drawn to the person who originally mirrored those traits for us.

Recognizing our feelings for others for what they are and not for what our conditioning has made them out to be is the key to mysteriously being drawn to another person. That unexplainable feeling that we have when we are with them—that magnetism and fire that makes us feel so alive—is really us! It is the essence of those parts of ourselves that we have lost, and our recognition that we want them back in our lives.

## RECOGNIZING WHAT YOU'VE LOST IN OTHER PEOPLE: AN EXERCISE

Each of us has masterfully given away the portions of ourselves that we felt were necessary in the moment for our physical or emotional survival. When we do so, it is easy to see ourselves as "less than" and get trapped within our beliefs of what remains. For some people, the trade-off happens before we ever know it, and we don't realize what has happened. For others, it is a conscious choice.

When you do encounter someone in your life who ignites a feeling of familiarity, I invite you to immerse yourself in the moment. Something rare and precious is happening for both of you. You have just found someone who has kept the pieces of you for which you are searching. Often this is a two-way experience, with the other person being drawn to you for the same reason!

Using your power of discernment, if you feel that it is appropriate, initiate a conversation. Begin talking about anything, anything at all, to maintain eye contact. While you are speaking, in your mind ask yourself this simple question: *What do I see in this person that I have lost in myself, given away, or had taken by those who have power over me?* Almost immediately, a response will come to your mind. It may be something as simple as a feeling of realization, or as clear as a voice within that you recognize and that has been with you since childhood.

Answers are often single words or short phrases. Your body knows what is meaningful for you. Maybe you simply recognize a beauty in this person that you feel is missing within you for the moment. Possibly it will be the person's innocence in life, the grace with which the person moves down the grocery aisle, the person's confidence as he performs the task at hand, or simply the radiance of his vitality.

Your encounter need last only seconds, perhaps a few minutes at most. Those brief moments are your opportunity to feel the joy and exhilaration of the moment. This is you, finding something of yourself in another person, something that you already have—and the feeling of what it is like to have that something awakened.

For those who dare to acknowledge the feeling of familiarity in such momentary encounters, the mirror of loss is probably something that faces them every day. We find that completeness in ourselves as others mirror to us our truest nature. Collectively, we are looking for our wholeness. Individually, we create the situations that lead us to find it. From clergy and teachers to older people watching youthful people, like parents watching their children, all are catalysts of feeling.

In those feelings, we find the things we long for in ourselves, the things that are still with us yet hidden in our masks of who we believe we are. It is natural. It is human. Understanding what your feelings about others are really saying about you may become your most powerful tool in discovering your greatest power.

## HOW TO USE PARABLE 1

Read this parable silently, or out loud. As you read each phrase, contemplate how the theme of this ancient parable may be a metaphor that relates to your life today. Silently ask yourself the following questions:

- Do I recognize a parallel between the woman carrying the jar of meal on the road and me as a human vessel carrying love, trust, and faith on my journey through life?

- Just as the woman didn't notice the meal slowly draining from the jar she was carrying, have I lost, given away, or had pieces of myself taken by those with power over me or my energy sapped by responding to the needs of my family and clients, gradually over time, and not noticed my loss?

- When the woman reached in the jar for the meal, the jar was empty. Have I given away so much of myself over the course of my life— drained my emotional vessel—that it's now difficult for me to love fully and completely when I really want to?

- How do I go about reclaiming the parts of myself that I've lost, given away, or had taken from me by those who had, or still have, power over me?

Make it a point to become mindful of the people whom you feel good being around.

# Notes

_____

_____

_____

_____

_____

_____

_____

_____

_____

_____

_____

_____

_____

_____

# Notes

_____

_____

_____

_____

_____

_____

_____

_____

_____

_____

_____

_____

_____

# parable 2

## The Poison Arrow

PARABLE 2: The parable of the poison arrow

USE: This wisdom code reminds us of the practical benefit of dealing immediately with the conditions that life presents to us, rather than waiting for the achievement of preconditions that may never be met.

SOURCE: The Parable of the Poison Arrow, discourse from the Buddhist Sutta Pitaka

The Parable of the Poison Arrow describes a hypothetical situation that forms the basis for a well-known cautionary tale in the Buddhist community. Tradition states that Buddha offered this parable in response to repeated questions about topics that he felt were unnecessary to explore and irrelevant to ponder. When asked by a monk to respond to a series of philosophical questions regarding the nature of life, the cosmos, reality, and human existence, in this discourse the Buddha declines to address every single one of these topics due to the unknowable nature of the answers. The text known as the Sabbasava Sutta (or Sutra) identifies the 16 questions that the monk asked as follows:

> *What am I? How am I? Am I? Am I not? Did I exist in the past? Did I not exist in the past? What was I in the past? How was I in the past? Having been what, did I become what in the past? Shall I exist in future? Shall I not exist in future? What shall I be in future? How shall I be in future? Having been what, shall I become what in future? Whence came this person? Whither will he go?*

When Buddha is pressed to respond to the monk's query, he does so by stating that it is a waste of time to ponder these esoteric questions. The Parable of the Poison Arrow is Buddha's way of illustrating why he feels the way he does and the reasoning underlying his answer.

In the book *Zen Keys*, Buddhist scholar Thich Nhat Hanh shares this version of the Poison Arrow parable:

> *Suppose a man is struck by a poisoned arrow and the doctor wishes to take out the arrow immediately. Suppose the man does not want the arrow removed until he knows who shot it, his age, his parents, and why he shot it. What*

*would happen? If he were to wait until all these questions have been answered, the man might die first.*

## WHAT DOES THIS PARABLE MEAN?

In this concise parable we are reminded of three factors that sometimes stand between us and realizing our dreams, desires, goals, and potentials:

- We sometimes create diversions that distract us from making important decisions and taking timely and meaningful action in life.

- By procrastinating when it comes to making our decisions, we sometimes create conditions that are worse that the initial situation we are avoiding.

- The consequence of delaying a difficult decision is that we give ourselves fewer options to choose among.

Let's take the parable step by step now. To illustrate his thinking, Buddha offers this hypothetical story. He proposes that a man walking along a path is suddenly struck by a poison arrow fired from the bow of an unseen and unknown archer. The wound is serious. The man is bleeding badly, and he is taken to a doctor to remove the arrow and stop the loss of blood.

## Diversions

In the presence of the doctor, however, the man delays the procedure by identifying factors that must be addressed—diversions masked as questions—*before* the arrow is removed. The questions that he asks, however, cannot be answered quickly. The man first wants the identity of the man who fired the arrow. Then he wants to know the age of the archer, the background of the archer's family, and finally, why he alone was targeted.

## Procrastination

While the questions the man is asking are reasonable, and the answers to the questions may be informative, and even interesting, they are not necessary. The doctor does not need the answers to remedy the immediate threat and remove the arrow that's embedded in the man's body. The questioning allows the man to put off what is sure to be a painful process—to procrastinate when it comes to the procedure of removing the arrow.

## Consequences

Because the answers cannot be known in the present moment, and the mysteries of the archer solved, the consequence of delaying the procedure puts the man's life in increasing danger. The prudent thing to do is to remedy the danger and remove the arrow immediately so that the healing can begin. The consequence of failing to do so will lead to more bleeding and eventually the man's death.

As is often the case with a parable, the story makes a point, but it doesn't tell us how the situation ends. We don't get to know if the arrow is removed, or if the man survives his insistence on having the information first.


## Our Question

How often do we find ourselves creating diversions to delay making a difficult decision in our lives? How often do we justify delaying a choice by insisting that more data is needed to act on a choice that we've already made intuitively? And how often do we discover that the situations of our relationships, health, and jobs become more difficult, and even more complex, because of our procrastination?

From personal issues of intimacy to global issues such as climate change, we experience diversions that delay our choices almost on a daily basis. How much more information do we need, for example, to tell us we're in an unhealthy relationship before we choose to do something healthy for ourselves and leave the relationship? How many ice core studies and sea level measurements do we need to do before we accept that climate change is a fact and we need to adapt to the changes ASAP? In such situations, we're like the man who's been shot by the arrow. We don't need to know the background details or understand the entire history of the circumstances that are creating stress in our life. We don't need to know about an abusive partner's childhood, previous relationships, or health challenges to know that what is happening in the moment isn't good for us. And while the sources of climate change may be in dispute for another quarter century, we don't need the history to know that we need to adapt now.

And like the man with the arrow, while we're procrastinating the removal of the "poison" from a bad relationship or failure to act on climate change, we may succumb to the poison before we feel complete in our diversions. And like the man with the poison arrow as well, the sooner we remove the poison from our lives, the sooner our healing can begin.

## HOW TO USE PARABLE 2

Read this parable silently, or out loud. After creating a focus in your heart (see "How to Use the Wisdom Codes," on page xix), silently ask yourself the following questions:

- Do I recognize a parallel between the man who was struck with the arrow, the way he created diversions in his life to delay the pain of removing the arrow from his body, and the way that I'm addressing difficult decisions in my life right now?

- What issue/issues/people in my life are poisoning my health, dreams, and desires like the poison arrow in this parable?

- What are the consequences of my procrastination?

- What are the best options available to take responsibility for my situation and the decisions that face me today?

Make it a point to become mindful of the answers that come to you when you ask these questions from the one-mind of your heart, rather than from the polarity of your mind.

# ACKNOWLEDGMENTS

*The Wisdom Codes* marks my ninth book as a Hay House author. My writing of the book, however, was only the beginning of the cooperative process that makes it possible for me to share this book with you. Through a process that most readers will never see, a dedicated community of copyeditors, proof editors, graphic designers, social media, marketing, and publicity strategists, event producers, sales representatives, book distributors, and bookstore buyers had to arrange their schedules around my promise that *The Wisdom Codes* would be ready when I promised. Although I will never meet most of this community personally, I know they're there, and I'm deeply honored to share our journey. I'm eternally thankful for all that they do each day to share the information, insights, techniques, and human stories that make this world a better place. I would like to take this opportunity to express my gratitude to those whose efforts have directly contributed to making this book possible. Specifically, I want to express my gratitude:

To Louise Hay for her unwavering belief in our potential to heal, and to love ourselves into healing, and for expressing her vision as the extraordinary family that has become Hay House. Though Louise left the world before this book was completed, her intuitive philosophies laid the foundation for writing *The Wisdom Codes*.

To Reid Tracy, for your vision and personal dedication to the truly extraordinary way of doing business that has become the hallmark of Hay House's success, and especially for your support, rock-solid advice, and your trust in me and my work for 16 years—I look forward to seeing where the next 16 years lead us!

To Margarete Nielsen, COO, for your vision, dedication, and leadership. I'm especially grateful for your sage advice that opens a window from my personal desk in New Mexico into the big, ever-changing world of media and publishing, your trust in me and my decisions, and your always-present friendship and support.

To Patty Gift, Vice President and Publisher. Who could have known when you introduced me to Harmony Books in 1999 where our journey would lead? Thank you for your trust, advice, wisdom, and support over two decades of life shifts and world changes. Most of all, thank you for your unwavering friendship.

To Anne Barthel, Editorial Director for Hay House U.S. I'm honored and blessed to know you as my most amazing and talented all-around literary guru, most awesome editor, trusted sounding board, and now as my dear friend.

To each and every one of the greatest group of people I could ever imagine working with, the many members of our global Hay House family, among them: Sergio Garcia and all of the members of our web team; Alexandra Israel, Senior Publicist and my worldwide publicist extraordinaire; Lindsay McGinty, Associate Director of Publicity and Book Marketing and my own big-picture-of-the-world publicity manager; Tricia Breidenthal, Art Director, and her staff of patient and gifted designers and artists; Rocky George, the perfect audio engineer, with the ear for just the right sound; and Melissa Brinkerhoff, Director of Customer Care, for always being there for me and my office to support us as we try new models for sharing the ideas in my books and for the perfectly stocked book tables at our conferences—you're all absolutely the very best! I couldn't ask for a more awesome group of people to work with or a more dedicated team to support my work. Your excitement and professionalism are unsurpassed, and I'm proud to be a part of all the good things that the Hay House family brings to our world.

I am grateful to Ned Leavitt, my one-and-only literary agent—thank you so very much for your wisdom, integrity, and the human touch that you bring to every milestone we cross together. Through your guidance in shepherding our books through the ever-changing world of publishing, we have reached countless people in over 70 countries on six continents with our empowering message of hope and possibility. While I deeply appreciate your impeccable guidance, I am especially grateful for your trust in me and our friendship.

My heartfelt gratitude and deepest appreciation for Stephanie Gunning, my first-line editor extraordinaire for 16 years, and through it all, still my dear friend. You have my deepest respect for your knowledge of the world, your impeccable language skills, and your ability to treat each of our books as if it's our first, and my gratitude for the way you generously shower your gifts onto each of our projects.

I am proud to be part of the virtual team, and the family, that has grown around the support of my work over the years, including Lauri Willmot, my dear friend and confidant since 1996 and now the Executive Director of our company, Wisdom Traditions. I admire your strength, wisdom, and clear thinking, respect you deeply, and appreciate the countless ways that you're there for me, always, and especially when it counts. I look forward to the new journey that we've embarked upon and the mystery of where it will lead us. You can't retire until I do!

Thank you, Rita Curtis, my business manager extraordinaire, and now my friend: I deeply appreciate your vision, your clarity, and your skills that get us from here, to there, each month. Most of all, I appreciate your trust, your openness to new ideas, and especially our growing friendship.

To Elan Cohen, the most awesome event producer, live event director, and now, my dear friend. Thank you for your visionary skills, your trust in me, your openness to my ideas, and the joy that continues to say "yes!" to the journey that we began over 15 years ago.

To my mother, Sylvia, who supported my early passion for science, art, and music even when she didn't understand them; and my younger brother, Eric, for your unfailing love and for always believing in me. Though our blood family is small, together we have found that our extended family of love is greater than we could have imagined. Thank you for all that you bring to my life each day.

To my beautiful wife, Martha, thank you for your lasting friendship, gentle wisdom, and all-embracing love that is with me each day of my life. Along with Woody "Bear," our new little Willow, and our recently departed Nemo, the furry beings we share our lives with, you are the family that gives me the reason to come home from each event. Thank you for all that you bring to my life.

A very special thanks to everyone who has supported my work, books, recordings, and live presentations over the years. I am honored by your trust, in awe of your vision for a better world, and deeply appreciative of your passion for bringing that world into existence. Through your presence, I have learned to become a better listener and heard the words that allow me to share our empowering message of hope and possibility. To all, I remain grateful in all ways, always.

# REFERENCES

## Epigraphs

*"A single word has the power to influence the expression of genes . . ."* Andrew Newberg, M.D., and Mark Robert Waldman, *Words Can Change Your Brain: 12 Conversation Strategies to Build Trust, Resolve Conflicts, and Increase Intimacy* (New York: Hudson Street Press, 2012), 3.

*"I know nothing in the world that has as much power as a word."* Emily Dickinson, Letters.

## Introduction

Benjamin Lee Whorf, "Science and Linguistics," first published in *MIT Technology Review* 42, no. 6 (April 1940): 229–31; reprinted in *Language, Thought, and Reality: Selected Writings of Benjamin Lee Whorf,* ed. John B. Carroll (Cambridge, MA: The MIT Press, Massachusetts Institute of Technology, 1956), 212–214. Benjamin Lee Whorf died from cancer in 1941 before he had the opportunity to publish a complete version of his theories. Although he successfully published a series of papers before his death, including the aforementioned article, the definitive representations of his work were published posthumously by colleagues such as G. L. Trager, who published the definitive paper "The Systematization of the Whorf Hypothesis." This is among the papers that are typically used to reference Whorf's ideas today.

Roberto Cazzolla Gatti, "A Conceptual Model of New Hypothesis on the Evolution of Biodiversity," *Biologia* 71, no. 3 (March 2016): 343, https://doi.org/10.1515/biolog-2016-0032. The best science of the 21st century has overturned 150 years of thinking based upon Charles Darwin's model for the fundamental principle of natural systems. In fact, nature is based upon cooperation, not competition.

*"A single word has the power to influence the expression of genes . . ."* Andrew Newberg, M.D., and Mark Robert Waldman. *Words Can Change Your Brain: 12 Conversation Strategies to Build Trust, Resolve Conflicts, and Increase Intimacy* (New York: Hudson Street Press, 2012), 3. This landmark book supports the ideas that Benjamin Lee Whorf proposed earlier in the 20th century and takes the word-human relationship from the level of neurons deeper to the level of gene expression.

*"Over time the structure of your thalamus will also change . . ."* Andrew Newberg, M.D., and Mark Robert Waldman, in "Words Can Change Your Brain," Therese J. Borchard, PsychCentral.com, May 27, 2019, https://psychcentral.com/blog/words-can-change-your-brain-2.

## How to Use the Wisdom Codes

The Quick Coherence Technique was developed by the HeartMath Institute, founded in 1991. It is based on three decades of important groundbreaking research in neurobiology that has led to new discoveries about the presence of neurons in the heart, heart/brain coherence, and the relationship between the human heart and the magnetic fields of the Earth.

For scientific details of heart/brain coherence, read the first two chapters in my book *Resilience from the Heart: The Power to Thrive in Life's Extremes* (Carlsbad, CA: Hay House, 2015). This book was originally released under the title *The Turning Point: Creating Resilience in a Time of Extremes* (2014). It was retitled to emphasize the techniques and applications of heart focus and heart-based coherence for personal resilience.

### The Words Are the Codes

*"Words can light fires in the minds of men . . ."* Patrick Rothfuss, *The Name of the Wind* (New York: DAW Books, 2007).

*"Whatsoever ye shall ask the Father in my name . . ."* John 16:23 (King James Version). In 1604, King James I of England commissioned a new translation of the Bible. Since its publication in 1611, this version has been the standard for many groups of English-speaking Protestants.

*"Ask without hidden motive and be surrounded by your answer . . ."* Neil Douglas-Klotz, translator, *Prayers of the Cosmos: Meditations on the Aramaic Words of Jesus* (San Francisco, CA: HarperSanFrancisco, 1994), 86–87.

*"Mountain, move away . . ."* "The Gospel of Thomas (II, 2)," Helmut Koester and Thomas O. Lambdin, in *The Nag Hammadi Library*, ed. James M. Robinson (New York: HarperCollins, 1990), 137. The scrolls known collectively as the Nag Hammadi Library—the oldest and most complete records known to exist of the New Testament texts—were discovered in 1945 in Egypt, only a year before the Dead Sea Scrolls were discovered in the caves of Qumran. The discovery was especially significant, as well as controversial, because the find revealed that many texts had been removed from the biblical canon used by the Catholic Church in the 4th century, including this gospel.

### Part One: Protection

Epigraph. "Craig D. Lounsbrough Quotes," Goodreads.com, accessed August 12, 2019.

### Wisdom Code 1: Psalm 91

Of the various translations of Psalm 91, I chose the English translation that is most widely accepted and accessible for the nonacademic readers, the King James Version.

*"Blessed be Abram by God Most High . . ."* Holy Bible: From the Ancient Eastern Text, George M. Lamsa's Translation from the Aramaic of the Peshitta, trans. George M. Lamsa (Philadelphia: A. J. Holman Company, 1933). The word *peshitta* means "common" in the Syriac language, and is the name given to a translation of the Christian Bible from around the 3rd century.

### Wisdom Code 2: Prayer of Refuge

Lobsang Wangdu, "How to Say the Refuge Prayer in Tibetan," YoWangdu.com, accessed August 19, 2019, https://www.yowangdu.com/tibetan-buddhism/refuge-prayer.html. The Tibetan Prayer of Refuge (*kyamdro*) is a traditional Buddhist prayer. While the theme of every translation I have read appears the same, nuances of interpretations are reflected in the various translations. For reasons of clarity and accuracy, for Wisdom Code 2 I've chosen a translation by Lobsang Wangdu. A Tibetan living in the United States, he was formerly a Buddhist monk and holds a master's degree in Madyamika from the Institute of Buddhist Dialectics in Dharamsala, India. Wangdu's blog post on kyamdro includes a video of him pronouncing the Prayer of Refuge in the Tibetan language.

### Wisdom Code 3: The Lord's Prayer

*"Our Father in heaven, hallowed be thy name. . ."* Holy Bible: From the Ancient Eastern Text, George M. Lamsa's Translation from the Aramaic of the Peshitta, trans. George M. Lamsa (Philadelphia: A. J. Holman Company, 1933). As is the case with so many of the wisdom codes, the words of the Lord's Prayer exist today in numerous translations that reflect people's various interpretations of this text. The Peshitta version of the Bible is the name given to a translation of the Christian Bible from the original Syriac dialect of Aramaic used around the 3rd century. I've chosen George M. Lamsa's translation of the Peshitta version of the Lord's Prayer because he was a native Aramaic speaker. This translation appears to be closer to the original language that Jesus would have used to reveal the prayer in his day.

# References

Burton L. Mack, *The Lost Gospel: The Book of Q and Christian Origins* (San Francisco: HarperOne, 2013).

*"This form of Aramaic is very similar to, . . ."* Stephen Andrew Missick, "The Lord's Prayer in the Original Aramaic," *Aramaic Herald*, March 18, 2011, http://aramaicherald. blogspot.com/2011/03/lords-prayer-in-original-aramaic-by.html.

This quote is from a portion of his blog that summarizes his views and research contained in his book *The Language of Jesus: Introducing Aramaic* (Amazon Digital Services, LLC, 2010).

The Revised Standard Version (RSV) of the Bible was released in 1952 and does not include the Byzantine doxology, for the reasons described in Wisdom Code 3. The RSV uses both the King James Version and American Standard Version as its primary source texts. The purpose of the RSV was to make the Bible more readable for contemporary people by removing words that are no longer commonly used, such as *thou*, *thee*, and *speaketh*, while honoring the original intent and theme of the text.

*"The doxology . . . appears later for the first time in the Didache . . ."* The doxology is absent in the book of Luke, and in the Revised Standard Version of the Lord's Prayer, Matthew 6:9–13. It first appears in the Didache text (circa 1 c.e.), as part of what are considered to be the second-generation Christian writings.

*"Abwoon d'bwashmaya . . ."* Neil Douglas-Klotz, translator, *Prayers of the Cosmos: Meditations on the Aramaic Words of Jesus* (San Francisco: HarperSanFrancisco, 1994). While there are many possible translations and layers of meaning associated with the Aramaic language, I've favored and often relied upon this particular translation since it was first released in 1990. I'm including it here as a reference for the Lord's Prayer, as well as other significant works such as the Aramaic translation of the Beatitudes.

## Wisdom Code 4: Gayatri Mantra

*"Brahma, the manifestation of spiritual energy . . ."* Swami Vivekananda, *The Complete Works of the Swami Vivekananda, Volume One* (Advaita Ashram, 2016). This first volume in a nine-volume set celebrates the 150th anniversary of Swami Vivekananda's birth in 1863 and offers a deeper exploration of the traditional Hindu mantras, including the Gayatri.

*"O thou existence Absolute, Creator of the three dimensions. . ."* Shri Gyan Rajhans. "The Gayatri Mantra." Learn Religions, June 12, 2019, https://www.learnreligions.com/the-gayatri-mantra-1770541.

The age of the Vedas is uncertain. Scholars commonly attribute the origin of the Rig Veda, the oldest of the Vedas, to a date of approximately 1100–1700 b.c.e. Some scholars, however, suggest that the texts may have originated as long as 7,000 years ago. As with many texts of such antiquity, there are many translations, based upon many interpretations of the original text. While I have chosen the beautiful and precise translation of Kumud Ajmani, Ph.D., for Wisdom Code 4, other translations are available and may vary in their specifics.

*"Aum Bhur Bhuvah Swah . . ."* Kumud Ajmani, "Gayatri Mantra Word by Word Meaning," Glimpses of Divinity: The EagleSpace Blog, January 25, 2018, https://blog.eaglespace.com/gayatri-mantra-words. This discussion of the Gayatri Mantra is one of the best, most concise, and accurate that I've come across in my research.

## Part Two: Fear

Epigraph. Pema Chödrön, *When Things Fall Apart: Heart Advice for Difficult Times* (Boston: Shambhala Publications, 1997), 22.

Candace Pert, *Molecules of Emotion: The Science Behind Mind-Body Medicine* (New York: Simon and Schuster, 1999). I had the privilege of meeting and getting to know Pert before she died in 2013. We were both publishing and distributing our books through Hay House, and the I Can Do It conferences of the time were tremendous opportunities for speakers to meet and support one another's work. I have tremendous respect for her paradigm-altering work documenting the body's production of chemicals (neuropeptides) from emotional experiences and the role of unresolved emotion and trauma in hindering the body's ability to metabolize these chemicals.

Karl Albrecht, "The (Only) 5 Fears We All Share," *Psychology Today* blog, March 22, 2012. The fear of annihilation is first on the list of the five fears that we share universally as humans. A psychologist, Albrecht concisely identifies and describes these fears and the role they play in our lives.

The law of conservation of energy is a fundamental principle of thermodynamics. Rather than being a discovery that occurred in a moment in time, recognition of this physical law evolved gradually over centuries, with roots in the observations of astronomer and physicist Galileo in the 1600s. In 1842, Julius Robert von Mayer formalized the principle in the expression that "energy can be neither created, nor destroyed." This is a key concept when it comes to the consideration of human immortality and the ultimate fate of the energy of the soul.

## Wisdom Code 5: Katha Upanishad

*"The soul is not born, nor does it die . . ."* Swami Mukundananda, "Bhagavad Gita: Chapter 2, Verse 20," Bhagavad Gita: The Song of God, accessed August 9, 2019, https://www.holy-bhagavad-gita.org/chapter/2/verse/20.

While the words of Wisdom Code 5 are found in the Upanishad as described in the text, a nearly identical version is also found in the Bhagavad Gita, chapter 2, verse 20: "The soul is neither born, nor does it ever die; nor having once existed, does it ever cease to be. The soul is without birth, eternal, immortal, and ageless. It is not destroyed when the body is destroyed."

## Wisdom Code 6: Pyramid Texts

R. O. Faulkner, *The Ancient Egyptian Pyramid Texts* (Stilwell, KS.: Digireads.com, 2007), 42. This 1969 translation is my primary source for this chapter. Of the many and varied translations that are now available for the Pyramid Texts, I've found British Egyptologist Faulkner's to be the most accurate, concise, and consistent with the translations that I received from the Egyptian guides who first led me into the chambers below the Unas Pyramid in 1986. Faulkner contributed to the translation of the Pyramid Texts that is available as an accompaniment to images of the hieroglyphics, chamber by chamber, online at https://www.pyramidtextsonline.com/translation.html.

## Wisdom Code 7: Bhagavad Gita

Swami Mukundananda, trans. and commentary, *Bhagavad Gita: The Song of God* (Dallas: Jagadguru Kripaluji Yog, 2017). This is my primary source for this chapter.

*"The soul is never created, nor does it ever die . . ."* Mukundananda, "Bhagavad Gita: Chapter 2, Verse 20," accessed August 9, 2019, https://www.holy-bhagavad-gita.org/chapter/2/verse/20.

*"That which pervades the entire body . . ."* Mukundananda, "Bhagavad Gita: Chapter 2, Verse 17," accessed August 9, 2019, https://www.holy-bhagavad-gita.org/chapter/2/verse/17.

*"Weapons cannot shred the soul . . ."* Mukundananda, "Bhagavad Gita: Chapter 2, Verse 23," https://www.holy-bhagavad-gita.org/chapter/2/verse./23.

*"The soul is unbreakable and incombustible. . ."* Mukundananda, "Bhagavad Gita: Chapter 2, Verse 24," https://www.holy-bhagavad-gita.org/chapter/2/verse/24.

## Wisdom Code 8: The Gospel of Peace

*"One day your body will return to the Earthly Mother . . ."* Edmond Bordeaux Szekely, *The Essene Gospel of Peace: Book One* (Baja California: International Biogenic Society, 1981). As a young man, Szekely was sent to study at the Vatican in Rome. Around

1923 he was given access to the private Vatican Library, where he discovered the Aramaic gospel of Jesus's teachings. While he was not allowed to remove the documents from the library, he was allowed to transcribe them. Book One is the first of the four books that resulted from Bordeaux's translations.

*"Our 'Mother Earth' and our 'Father in Heaven' . . ."* Szekely, 56–7.

*"And you shall be one with the Holy Stream of Light . . ."* Szekely, 58.

## Part Three: Loss

Epigraph. "Norman Cousins Quotes," BrainyQuote.com, BrainyMedia Inc., accessed August 12, 2019, https://www.brainyquote.com/quotes/norman_cousins_121747.

*"Nature abhors a vacuum."* Aristotle, *Physics, Book IV*, chapters 6–9 (circa 350 B.C.E.).

Gregg Braden, *Secrets of the Lost Mode of Prayer: The Hidden Power of Beauty, Blessing, Wisdom and Hurt* (Carlsbad, CA: Hay House, 2006), 173–7.

## Wisdom Code 9: Otagaki Rengetsu

Otagaki Rengetsu, trans. John Stevens, *Rengetsu: Life and Poetry of Lotus Moon* (Brattleboro, VT: Echo Point Books and Media, 2014), 32. The Buddhist principle of impermanence that is the foundation of Wisdom Code 9 is described poetically in the work of the 19th-century Buddhist nun Otagaki Rengetsu. This book is my source for her work.

For a detailed discussion of the *three marks of existence*, I recommend the work of Vietnamese Buddhist monk Thich Nhat Hahn, especially his book *The Heart of the Buddha's Teaching: Transforming Suffering into Peace, Joy, and Liberation* (New York: Harmony, 1999), 141. The Buddhist teachings exist as layers of increasingly deep and subtler meaning.

## Wisdom Code 10: Buddha

As I did in Wisdom Code 9, I refer you to the work of Vietnamese Buddhist monk Thich Nhat Hahn, *The Heart of the Buddha's Teaching: Transforming Suffering into Peace, Joy, and Liberation* (New York: Harmony Books, 1999).

*"What we experience as 'balance' is actually a temporary state of harmony . . ."* Gregg Braden, *The Divine Matrix: Bridging Time, Space, Miracles, and Belief* (Carlsbad CA.: Hay House, 2007), 187–9. For a discussion of how this principle often plays out in our lives, please see Part III.

## Wisdom Code 11: Pavamana Mantra

Swami Prabhavananda and Fredrick Manchester, *The Upanishads: Breath of the Eternal*, 2nd ed. (Hollywood, CA: Vedanta Press, 1975), 80. The Pavamana Mantra was written approximately 2,700 years ago as part of the Brihadaranyaka Upanishad. As one of the primary Upanishads of Hinduism, the Brihadaranyaka is specifically dedicated to the exploration and metaphysics of the human soul (atman). While the Sanskrit text has remained as a stable text, there are many and varied English translations available. For the purposes of this book, I've chosen this translation of the Pavamana Mantra.

For additional commentary on word meanings, refer to *Om Asato Maa Sad-Gamaya*; look at https://en.wikipedia.org/wiki/Pavamana_Mantra.

*"Transformation of the individual and their environment . . ."* John Campbell, as cited in Shira Atkins, "A Beginner's Guide to Essential Sanskrit Mantras," Sonima, August 21, 2015, https://www.sonima.com/yoga/sanskrit-mantras.

## Part Four: Strength

Epigraph. "Katherine Dunham Quotes," Goodreads.com, accessed August 11, 2019, https://www.goodreads.com/quotes/592751-go-within-every-day-and-find-the-inner-strength-so.

George Gurdjieff wrote a series of books chronicling his mysterious journey to find the hidden teachings that became the central focus of his life. He published the French edition of his book *Meetings with Remarkable Men: All and Everything* in 1960. It was translated into English in 1963 and released as the film *Meetings with Remarkable Men*, written and directed by Peter Brook, in 1979. Gurdjieff called this book the first in his "second series" of writings.

Alfredo Metere, "Does Free Will Exist in the Universe? (That Would Be a No.)," *Cosmos*, July 18, 2018, https://cosmosmagazine.com/physics/does-free-will-exist-in-the-universe-that-would-be-a-no. While the conversation regarding choice and free will is often relegated to philosophical texts, it also goes directly to the essence of why Part Four is so powerful. This beautifully and responsibly written exploration of this powerful concept in an easy-to-read format was penned by a senior research scientist at the International Computer Science Institute.

## Wisdom Code 12: Beauty Prayer

Shonto Begay, "Shonto Begay," *Indian Artist* 3, no. 1 (winter 1997), 52. The informal version of the Beauty Prayer that I chose to begin the chapter is one I saw expressed by native artist Shonto Begay in a New Mexico–based art magazine, *Indian Artist*. While the magazine appears to no longer be active, I'm including the reference here for clarity.

*"This powerful code forms the closing prayer of the Blessing Way Ceremony . . ."* For a detailed discussion of how the Navajo ceremonies are performed, please see the Navajo Song Ceremonial Complex: https://en.wikipedia.org/wiki/Navajo_song_ceremonial_complex.

*"The beauty that you live with . . ."* Mark Sublette, "Shonto Begay, Native American Painter," *Canyon Road Arts: The Complete Visitors Guide to Arts, Dining and the Santa Fe Lifestyle*, March 10, 2013.

The full-length English translation of the Beauty Prayer was produced by Robert S. Drake for Tom Holm, Ph.D., University of Arizona American Indian Graduate Studies Program, Native American Religions and Spirituality. Read online and listen to a recording of Wayne Wilson reading the prayer in the original Navajo tongue: "Walk in Beauty: Prayer from the Navajo People," Talking Feather: Lesson Plans about Native American Indians, accessed August 19, 2019, https://talking-feather.com/home/walk-in-beauty-prayer-from-navajo-blessing.

## Wisdom Code 13: Vedic Mantra

In writing this chapter, I relied primarily upon three articles.

Michael Ireland, "Meditation and Psychological Health and Functioning: A Descriptive and Critical Review," *Scientific Review of Mental Health Practice* 9, no. 1 (May 2012), 4–19. This paper describes a scientific evaluation and benefits of various meditation practices.

Jai Paul Dudeja, "Scientific Analysis of Mantra-Based Meditation and Its Beneficial Effects: An Overview," *International Journal of Advanced Scientific Technologies in Engineering and Management Sciences* 3, no. 6 (June 2017), 21–6. Modern science is taking the ancient science of mantras seriously as the physical, as well as physiological are now well-documented. This journal reference describes one of these studies.

Ramesh, "Om Namah Shivaya–Meaning and Its Significance," Vedicfeed, June 24, 2018, https://vedicfeed.com/om-namah-shivaya-meaning. The Vedic mantra *Om Namah Shivaya* is an ancient mantra and traditional chant. The author breaks down the syllables of the mantra and shows how they pair to the elements of nature and the seven chakras.

*"Mantras have a very specific effect on our mental, emotional, physical and spiritual states."* MartinSchmidtInAsia, "Enchanted Chanting: Experiencing Peace and Purity in the High School Classroom," Social Conscience and Inner Awakening blog, September 12, 2018, https://martinschmidtinasia.wordpress.com/2018/09/12/enchanted-chanting-experiencing-peace-and-purity-in-the-high-school-classroom/.

# References

*"Now I am become death, the destroyer of worlds . . ."* Swami Mukundananda, Bhagavad Gita: The Song of God, chapter 11, verses 31–33, https://www.holy-bhagavad-gita.org/chapter/11/verse/32.

## Wisdom Code 14: Psalm 23

*"The Lord is my shepherd . . ."* For my biblical reference of the 23rd Psalm, in this chapter I have chosen the New International Version (NIV) for the reasons described in the text. For a comparison of the NIV version of Psalm 23 to the English Standard Version (ESV), I recommend www.biblegateway.com/passage/?-search=Psalm+23&version=ESV;Niv.

*"I am the shepherd of the people who causes the truth to appear . . ."* Stan Rummel, "The Hammurabi Stele: Partially Retold in English," K. C. Hanson's Home Page, accessed August 27, 2019, http://www.kchanson.com/ANCDOCS/meso/hammurabi.html. This English translation a very readable version of the text from the ancient Hammurabi stele, a stone monument with a record of 282 laws imposed by the king of Babylon in 1754 B.C.E.

## Part Five: Love

Epigraph. Kate McGahan, *Only Gone from Your Sight: Jack McAfghan's Little Guide to Pet Loss and Grief* (Kate McGahan: 2018).

*"Your task is not to seek for love . . ."* Goodreads.com, accessed August 13, 2019, https://www.goodreads.com/quotes/1268078-your-task-is-not-to-seek-for-love-but-merely.

*"Forgiveness doesn't excuse what another person has done . . ."* Andrea Brandt, Ph.D., M.F.T., "How Do You Forgive Even When It Feels Impossible? (Part 1)," *Psychology Today*, September 2, 2014.

*"Blessed is the man who has suffered, and found life . . ."* Helmut Koester and Thomas O. Lambdin, "The Gospel of Thomas (II, 2)," in *The Nag Hammadi Library*, rev. ed., James M. Robinson, ed. (New York: HarperCollins, 1990), 132.

*"That which you have will save you if you bring it forth from yourselves . . ."* Koester and Lambdin, "The Gospel of Thomas (II, 2)," 134.

*"Through the power of love, we can let go of past history . . ."* "Ernest Holmes Quotes, AZ Quotes (accessed August 13, 2019), https://www.azquotes.com/author/6840-Ernest_Holmes.

*"By forgiving, you are accepting the reality of what happened . . ."* Brandt, "How Do You Forgive Even When It Feels Impossible? (Part 1)."

## Wisdom Code 15: Gospel of Thomas

*"I forgive them for killing my parents . . ."* Ofer Aderet. "Holocaust Survivor Known for Forgiving Nazis Dies at 85 on Trip to Auschwitz," *Haaretz*, July 4, 2019.

*"If you bring forth what is within you, what you bring forth will save you . . ."* Koester and Lambdin, "The Gospel of Thomas (II, 2)," 134.

## Part Six: The Power Codes

Epigraph. Yehuda Berg. "The Power of Words," HuffPost, November 27, 2011, https://www.huffpost.com/entry/the-power-of-words-b_716183.

## Power Code 1: I Will

*"What happens on earth is but a pale reflection . . ."* Michael Wise; Martin Abegg, Jr.; and Edward Cook, trans. and commentary, "The Songs of the Sabbath Sacrifice," in *The Dead Sea Scrolls: A New Translation* (New York: HarperSanFrancisco, 1996), 365.

*"We live in a world . . . which exists independently of us human beings . . ."* Alice Calaprice, ed. *The Expanded Quotable Einstein* (Princeton, N.J.: Princeton University Press, 2000), 220.

*"We had this old idea, that there is a universe out there..."* F. David Peat, *Synchronicity: The Bridge Between Matter and Mind* (New York: Bantam Books, 1987), 4.

*"Like vast space where nothing is lacking and nothing is in excess..."* Richard B. Clarke. *Hsin-Hsin Ming: Seng-ts'an, Third Zen Patriarch* (Buffalo, NY: White Pine Press, 2011), 11. The Hsin-Hsin Ming is attributed to Chien Chih Seng-ts'an, third Zen patriarch, in the 6th century.

*"Lord, if thou wilt, thou canst make me clean."* King James Version, Matthew 8:2–3.

### Power Code 2: I Am

*"I Am that I Am."* King James Version, Exodus 3:14. The words that God spoke to Moses in response to the question of his identity.

*"Thus shalt thou say unto the children of Israel..."* Exodus 3:15.

*"The Universal Field does not judge the appropriateness of what we give it to reflect..."* Braden, *The Divine Matrix*, 161–4. For an expanded discussion of our relationship to the scientifically acknowledged field of energy that connects all things, I refer you to my earlier work.

*"Mountain, move away' it will move away..."* Koester and Lambdin, "The Gospel of Thomas (II, 2)," 137.

### Part Seven: The Parables

Epigraph. Roger C. Schank. *Tell Me a Story: Narrative and Intelligence* (Evanston, IL: Northwestern University Press, 1995).

*"Additional examples of rock paintings discovered to have survived in caverns in Southern France..."* In 1994 explorers discovered a previously sealed cave in southern France, with 425 images on the cave walls depicting 14 different species of animals. Carbon dating suggests the images are at least 32,000 years old, making them the oldest documented cave images to date. Director Werner Herzog explored the Chauvet cave in his documentary film *Cave of Forgotten Dreams*.

### Parable 1: The Woman and the Jar

*"Who are we... but the stories we tell about ourselves..."* Scott Turow, *Ordinary Heroes* (New York: Grand Central Publishing, 2011), 6.

Filmmaker Werner Herzog captured images of the world's oldest known cave paintings in his outstanding 2010 documentary *Cave of Forgotten Dreams*, https://en.wikipedia.org/wiki/Cave_of_Forgotten_Dreams.

*"Humans are not ideally set up to understand logic..."* Schank, *Tell Me a Story*.

*"Refines the neural pathways that lead to skillful navigation of life's problems..."* Jonathan Gottschall, *The Storytelling Animal: How Stories Make Us Human* (New York: Mariner Books, 2012), 67.

*"These are the hidden words that the living Jesus spoke..."* Koester and Lambdin, "The Gospel of Thomas (II, 2)," 126.

*"The kingdom of the father is like a certain woman who was carrying a jar full of meal..."* Koester and Lambdin, "The Gospel of Thomas (II, 2)," 126.

*"And when you say, 'Mountain, move away,' it will move away..."* Koester and Lambdin, "The Gospel of Thomas (II, 2)," 137.

### Parable 2: The Poison Arrow

*"Suppose a man is struck by a poisoned arrow..."* Thich Nhat Hanh, *Zen Keys: A Guide to Zen Practice* (New York: Harmony, 1994), 42.

# RESOURCES

## How to Use the Wisdom Codes

For new discoveries regarding the human heart, and detailed instructions for heart-brain coherence, please see my 2014 release, *Resilience from the Heart*. Gregg Braden, *Resilience from the Heart: The Power to Thrive in Life's Extremes* (Hay House, Inc., 2014). pp. 1-80.

For access to the research, webinars, and technology supporting personal as well as global coherence, please see the official HeartMath website: www.heartmath.org.

## Wisdom Code 2

Lobsang Wangdu spent over 20 years as a monk training in Buddhist philosophy and holds a master's degree in Madyamika from the Institute of Buddhist Dialectics in Dharamsala, India. For an excellent audio tutorial in chanting the Tibetan prayer of refuge, I recommend his website video: https://www.yowangdu. com/tibetan-buddhism/refuge-prayer.html.

The great yogi Atiśa Dīpaṃkara Śrījñāna organized and distilled all 84,000 teachings of the Buddha into a single, seminal text. Geshe Sonam Rinchen, *Atisha's Lamp for the Path to Enlightenment*, tr. Ruth Sonam (Snowlion Publications, January 1, 1997).

## Wisdom Code 3

If you'd like to recite the Lord's Prayer using the original Aramaic words and pronunciation, an audio tutorial for the words is available online at https://abwoon.org/library/learn-aramaic-prayer/.

# ABOUT THE AUTHOR

GREGG BRADEN is a five-time *New York Times* best-selling author, scientist, and lecturer and is internationally renowned as a pioneer bridging modern science, ancient wisdom, and human potential. From 1979 to 1990 Gregg worked as a problem solver during times of crisis for Fortune 500 companies, including Cisco Systems (their first technical operations manager), Phillips Petroleum (computer geologist during the first oil embargo of 1979–80), and Martin Marietta Defense Systems during the Cold War (a liaison for the U.S. Space Command/Star Wars Defense Initiative). He continues problem-solving today as he merges modern science and the wisdom of our past to reveal real-world solutions to the issues that challenge our lives. His research has led to 12 award-winning books now published in over 40 languages.

Gregg is a member of visionary organizations and think tanks including the American Association for the Advancement of Science, the Steering Committee for the Global Coherence Initiative, and the Evolutionary Leadership Organization. He has presented his discoveries in over 30 countries on six continents, has 16 film credits, and has been invited to speak to the United Nations, Fortune 500 companies, and the U.S. military. In 2019, the United Kingdom's *Watkins Mind Body Spirit* journal listed Gregg among the top

100 of the "world's most spiritually influential living people" for the sixth consecutive year. He is the recipient of numerous awards, including the Illuminate Film Festival 2019 Conscious Visionary Award and the 2019 New Thought Walden Award, and he is a 2020 nominee for the prestigious Templeton Prize, established to honor "outstanding individuals who have devoted their talents to expanding our vision of human purpose and ultimate reality."

## Hay House Titles of Related Interest

*YOU CAN HEAL YOUR LIFE, the movie,*
starring Louise Hay & Friends
(available as an online streaming video)
www.hayhouse.com/louise-movie

*THE SHIFT, the movie,*
starring Dr. Wayne W. Dyer
(available as an online streaming video)
www.hayhouse.com/the-shift-movie

\*\*\*

*EVERYTHING IS HERE TO HELP YOU:*
*A Loving Guide to Your Soul's Evolution,* by Matt Kahn

*MORE BEAUTIFUL THAN BEFORE:*
*How Suffering Transforms Us,* by Steve Leder

*THE POWER OF LOVE: Connecting to the Oneness,*
by James Van Praagh

*UPLIFTING PRAYERS TO LIGHT YOUR WAY:*
*200 Invocations for Challenging Times,* by Sonia Choquette

All of the above are available at your local bookstore,
or may be ordered by contacting Hay House (see next page).

\*\*\*

We hope you enjoyed this Hay House book. If you'd like to receive our online catalog featuring additional information on Hay House books and products, or if you'd like to find out more about the Hay Foundation, please contact:

Hay House, Inc., P.O. Box 5100, Carlsbad, CA 92018-5100
(760) 431-7695 or (800) 654-5126
(760) 431-6948 (fax) or (800) 650-5115 (fax)
www.hayhouse.com® • www.hayfoundation.org

———

*Published in Australia by:* Hay House Australia Pty. Ltd.,
18/36 Ralph St., Alexandria NSW 2015
*Phone:* 612-9669-4299 • *Fax:* 612-9669-4144
www.hayhouse.com.au

*Published in the United Kingdom by:* Hay House UK, Ltd.,
The Sixth Floor, Watson House, 54 Baker Street, London W1U 7BU
*Phone:* +44 (0)20 3927 7290 • *Fax:* +44 (0)20 3927 7291
www.hayhouse.co.uk

*Published in India by:* Hay House Publishers India,
Muskaan Complex, Plot No. 3, B-2, Vasant Kunj, New Delhi 110 070
*Phone:* 91-11-4176-1620 • *Fax:* 91-11-4176-1630
www.hayhouse.co.in

———

<u>Access New Knowledge.</u>
<u>Anytime. Anywhere.</u>

Learn and evolve at your own pace
with the world's leading experts.

www.hayhouseU.com

# MEDITATE.
# VISUALIZE.
# LEARN.

*Get the* **Empower You**
Unlimited Audio *Mobile App*

## Get unlimited access to the entire Hay House audio library!

### You'll get:

- 500+ inspiring and life-changing **audiobooks**
- 200+ ad-free **guided meditations** for sleep, healing, relaxation, spiritual connection, and more
- Hundreds of audios **under 20 minutes** to easily fit into your day
- **Exclusive content** *only* for subscribers
- **New audios** added every week
- No credits, **no limits**

**Listen to the audio version of this book for FREE!**

★★★★★ **I ADORE this app.** I use it almost every day. Such a blessing. – Aya Lucy Rose

Scan me with **your phone camera!**

**HAY HOUSE**

# TRY FOR FREE!
Go to: hayhouse.com/listen-free